Contents

Eagles

Mike Unwin

BLOOMSBURY

LONDON · NEW DELHI · NEW YORK · SYDNEY

Bloomsbury Publishing

50 Bedford Square
London
WC1B 3DP
UK

1385 Broadway
New York
NY 10018
USA

www.bloomsbury.com

BLOOMSBURY and the Diana logo are trademarks of Bloomsbury Publishing Plc

First published 2016

© Mike Unwin, 2016
Photographs and Illustrations © as credited on page 127, 2015

Mike Unwin has asserted his right under the Copyright, Designs and Patents Act, 1988,
to be identified as Author of this work.

British Library Cataloging-in-Publication Data
A catalogue record for this book is available from the British Library.

Library of Congress Cataloguing-in-Publication data has been applied for.

ISBN: PB: 978-1-4729-2183-3
         ePub: 978-1-4729-214-0

2 4 6 8 10 9 7 5 3 1

Design by Rod Teasdale
Printed and bound in China by C&C Offset printing co., Ltd

To find out more about our authors and books visit www.bloomsbury.com. Here you will find extracts,
author interviews, details of forthcoming events and the option to sign up for our newsletters.

For all items sold, Bloomsbury Publishing will donate a minimum of 2% of the publisher's
receipts from sales of licensed titles to RSPB Sales Ltd, the trading subsidiary of the RSPB.
Subsequent sellers of this book are not commercial participators for the purpose of Part II
of the Charities Act 1992.

Meet the Eagles

Eagles are among the most impressive hunters of the animal world. Their predatory prowess and flying skills have imbued them with a mystique that runs deep in our culture, and has elevated them to emblems of freedom and power across the globe. At the same time we have long seen them as competition. Reviled as snatchers of livestock, many species have suffered at our hands – their decline accelerated by the damage and destruction we have wrought on the wild landscapes in which they live.

Two species are found in the British Isles: the Golden Eagle and the White-tailed Eagle. Both are among the largest and most impressive of the world's eagles, and both have earned our admiration and our hostility in equal measure. These two magnificent birds are the focus of this book.

What is an eagle?

Eagles, in lay terms, are big birds of prey. They belong, in scientific terms, to the Accipitridae family, along with hawks, buzzards and other mostly smaller birds of prey. Some eagles, including our two UK species, are very big indeed. Among the 60 species worldwide, however, there is considerable variation: the smallest are little bigger than a Woodpigeon; the largest have the wingspan of a kitchen table and the power to kill a deer.

Eagles occur on every continent except Antarctica, although all but 14 species are confined to Africa and Eurasia. As a group, they have adapted to a wide range of habitats, from grasslands and deserts to mountains, wetlands and tropical forests. Most subsist almost entirely on live prey, which they capture using powerful eyesight, great flying skills and lethal talons. Hunting behaviour varies from one eagle type to another. Some eagles are specialists that have evolved specific techniques for capturing a particular form of prey. Snake eagles (genus *Circaetus*), for example, prey on snakes and other reptiles. Others – usually those that live in areas of more limited resources – are generalists, with the versatility to take a

Above: The White-tailed Eagle gets its name for an obvious reason.

Opposite: A Golden Eagle is the essence of predatory power and poise.

Above: The Short-toed Eagle, seen here demonstrating its talent as a specialist predator on snakes, can be found across the Mediterranean region and southern Asia.

wide range of prey. Despite their killing prowess, many eagles will also turn to carrion, where available. All prey, living or dead, is torn apart using the sharp, hooked bill that is characteristic of all raptors and especially powerful in eagles.

Few birds live longer than eagles, with some species known to survive 30 years or more. Most mate for life, returning to the same nest – or eyrie – year after year. In some species, including the two UK birds, this structure may reach an enormous size. Two eggs is the normal clutch size for many, though often only one chick survives to maturity – the weaker often succumbing to the aggression of the stronger (see page 81). Young eagles take up to five years to reach breeding maturity, going through several different plumages en route. Females in virtually all species grow considerably large than males.

Most large eagles occupy the role of apex predator in their respective ecosystems. That is, they sit at the top of their food chain and – other than in exceptional

circumstances – do not fall prey to other animals. Indeed, in some parts of the world, including the UK, eagles are the most powerful of all predators. The basic laws of ecology dictate that apex predators can never be numerous or the food pyramid would become top-heavy and break down. Thus, while some species of eagle are widespread, their numbers are always necessarily lower than those of most other birds.

Eagles are mostly solitary. They seldom flock, other than when – in certain species – gathering at key migration bottlenecks or at local sources of abundant food. When breeding, a pair generally requires large tracts of territory where it may hunt and raise its young without competition from others of its own kind. Due to their low population size and sparse distribution, most eagles are highly vulnerable to persecution, disturbance and habitat loss, and – being slow breeders – damaged populations are slow to recover. It is thus hardly surprising that many species of eagle around the world are under threat. Some, indeed, are highly endangered.

Above: A White-tailed Eagle joins two Steller's Sea Eagles off the frozen coast of northern Japan; sea eagles are unusual among eagles in that they often gather at abundant food sources.

Girl power: sexual dimorphism in eagles

In most birds of prey, the female is larger than the male. This size difference is especially pronounced among the larger *Aquila* eagles: a female Golden Eagle's wingspan is some 10% greater than her mate's and she generally weighs some 40% more. It is less pronounced in *Haliaeetus* eagles, such as the White-tailed Eagle, but females may still weigh up to 25% more than males. A similar disparity occurs in some other raptorial birds, including owls and skuas.

Scientists call this phenomenon 'reversed size dimorphism' ('reversed' because in most birds and mammals where one sex is larger than the other, it is generally the male). The reasons are not fully understood. Predators that hunt agile prey tend to be most successful when they are roughly the same size as their quarry; it thus makes sense for males – who do most of the hunting during the breeding season – to be smaller than their mates. Meanwhile a greater size allows females to build

Above: These two mating Golden Eagles in Finland illustrate the disparity in size between the larger female (below) and the smaller male.

up body reserves more efficiently in preparation for breeding and also makes them more fearsome defenders of the nest. When not breeding, the size disparity means that male and female take different prey. This prevents them from competing with one another and means they can sustain a smaller territory.

With no other visible difference between male and female eagles, size difference can help distinguish the two in the field. This is most appreciable when they are soaring side by side, especially with Golden Eagles. Otherwise, sexing the bird in the hand involves a complicated formula calculated from the length of the hallux (hind claw) and culmen (top line of the bill). And, frankly, these are not birds that you generally want in your hand.

Two of our own

Britain's two eagle species are rare birds in our country, both confined almost entirely to the remote Scottish Highlands and Islands. Any sighting is sure to count among our most exciting and sought-after wildlife experiences. Both species do, however, have a worldwide distribution that extends far beyond the UK. Wherever you see one, whether at home or abroad, even a half-decent view generally leaves little doubt that what you are seeing is an eagle. Both species tick all the basic eagle boxes: they are huge, brown, live only in wild places and are most often seen soaring high in the sky – dwarfing any smaller bird that approaches them. A closer view, should you be so lucky, also reveals the massive bills and talons, and that imperious, heavy-browed, 'don't mess with me' glare.

Above: In the UK the Golden Eagle is largely a bird of inland mountains.

Despite these similarities, however, our two species are not closely related – they belong to separate genera – and differ significantly in both appearance and lifestyle. While both are massive birds, the Golden Eagle is slightly smaller than the White-tailed, which has a more vulture-like silhouette, a more ponderous flight and, in adults, a distinctive white tail. Furthermore, the Golden Eagle occurs largely inland, breeding on remote cliffs and mountainsides, where it hunts prey such as hares and game birds. By contrast, the White-tailed Eagle, which conservationists

Above: In the UK the White-tailed Eagle mostly frequents coastlines and offshore islands.

reintroduced to the UK in the 1970s (see page 119), occurs along the coast, where it feeds largely on fish and water birds. Golden Eagles are much the more numerous of the two species, with some 440 breeding pairs compared with no more than 100 of the White-tailed. Nonetheless, Golden Eagles are more retiring birds and sightings are less predictable than those of White-tailed Eagles, which tend to make themselves more obvious in the few places where they occur.

Meet the Golden Eagle

Above: The Golden Eagle's imperious profile makes it well suited to heraldic imagery.

Ask the average child in the UK to name one kind of eagle and the chances are that the answer will be 'Golden'. This regal bird is, for many people across the northern hemisphere, the definitive eagle. It is enshrined as the national emblem of five nations (see page 101), which makes it arguably the most popular national animal in the world. It was the standard under which the Roman legions marched as they conquered most of Europe (see page 102), and is the 'Eagle' of Tennyson's celebrated poem (see page 112).

Size and appearance

The Golden Eagle (*Aquila chrysaetos*) is the biggest species in the *Aquila* genus of eagles, otherwise known as the 'booted' or 'true' eagles. Among all eagles worldwide it is, on average, the seventh heaviest and has the fifth broadest wingspan. Females are some 20–30 per cent bigger than males. In the UK, the average male weighs 3.7kg (8lb) and the average female 5.2kg (11½lb) – the weight of a large house cat. The average male has a wingspan of 2.0m (6½ft) and the average female 2.2m (7ft). British Golden Eagles are not the biggest of their kind, however. Scientists recognise up to six races of this species around the world, which differ appreciably in size (see page 34).

Right: A Golden Eagle gets its name from the golden feathers on its nape.

Adult Golden Eagles are essentially dark brown. They have a sandy nape that flashes gold in sunlight – hence the name – and areas of paler grey on the wings and tail. Races vary: the European is generally the palest, and has more golden colouration extending onto the back; other races are darker or more reddish tinged. Immatures of all races have striking patches of white on the primary wing feathers and tail, which gradually shrink as a bird matures and have usually disappeared by its fifth year. Other key features of this species are the bright yellow legs and yellow cere – the skin at the base of the bill.

Above: White feathers in the wings and tail show that this Golden Eagle is an immature.

In the field, however, it is by shape rather than colour that you are most likely to identify a Golden Eagle. Its long neck and massive bill are more prominent than those of smaller brown raptors, such as the Common Buzzard, and in flight protrude appreciably further – as does the tail. Its head is less prominent than that of a White-tailed Eagle but its tail is longer. The massive wings are more graceful in their contours than the White-tailed Eagle's. When soaring they are spread in a shallow 'V' – or dihedral – unlike those of any other raptor of the same size, with the primary tips splayed like fingers. When gliding they may be swept back, with the fingers closed, and when diving they may be held tight against the body, with the huge 'shoulders' bulging forwards on either side of the head.

Perched, the bird's physique radiates muscular power, with massive 'shoulders' (in reality, the wrist joint of the folded wing) that protrude in front of the deep chest. A good view of a perched bird shows shaggy 'trousers' and a lower leg – tarsus – that is feathered right down to the toes. This feathered tarsus is characteristic of all *Aquila* eagles (hence 'booted') and a feature that distinguishes them from sea eagles, including the White-tailed Eagle.

Where to see one

In Britain the Golden Eagle is confined almost entirely to Scotland, where it inhabits the wild mountains and glens of the Highlands, from east to west, and also some of the Hebrides, including the islands of Skye, Mull and Islay, and the larger islands of the Outer Hebrides. A relict, isolated population in England's Lake District has for some years now consisted of just a single lonely male.

Above: The maps above show the Golden Eagle's worldwide range and (inset map) its range within Europe. Green shows where it is resident year-round; yellow shows where it is present only during the summer breeding season; blue shows where it is present only as a winter visitor.

A recent reintroduction programme aims to re-establish Golden Eagles in Ireland, where they died out in 1912.

Beyond our shores the Golden Eagle enjoys a wide distribution right across the northern hemisphere, although nowhere is it numerous. In continental Europe it inhabits mountainous regions, from the Iberian Peninsula through the Pyrenees and Alps to eastern Europe and across Scandinavia, with the biggest populations in Spain (c. 1,000 pairs) and Norway (c. 800 pairs). In Asia it occurs across Russia and China, east to Japan and south to Turkey (c. 2,000 pairs), the Caucasus, the Himalayas and the central steppes. In the Middle East and north Africa, it breeds in the mountains of Israel, Oman, Morocco and Tunisia, with isolated populations in Niger, Mali and the Bale Mountains of Ethiopia – its southernmost breeding limit. In North America, which has the largest population, at an estimated 70,000– 100,000 breeding pairs, it occurs from Mexico up through the western United States and across Canada.

Wherever in the world it lives, the Golden Eagle has similar habitat requirements – namely large, undisturbed tracts of open country, generally with cliffs or escarpments on which to nest. In much of its range, including Scotland, it is associated with mountains, hunting on moorland or alpine pasture. Indeed, in the Himalayas it has been recorded at more than 6,000m (19,685ft). High altitude, however, is not a prerequisite, and this bird occurs in lowland regions where conditions are right, such as on the edge of the Arctic tundra and in arid semi-desert, prairie and steppe. It tends to avoid dense forest, but occurs in more thinly treed areas, such as the fringes of the taiga forests of Russia and Scandinavia, and the dry oak woodlands of Mexico and California.

Above: Golden Eagles prefer open terrain, which better suits their hunting techniques.

The Golden Eagle is a partial migrant, which means that it migrates in some areas of its range but in other areas – where resources remain more constant – it tends to stay put. Migrant populations tend to be those that breed at latitudes greater than 60° N, where winters are severe and food is hard to find. Immature birds travel further and disperse more widely than do adults. In the UK, winter sees many Scottish birds descend to the lowlands and coast, and south into the Borders.

Food and hunting

Typical prey for the Golden Eagle comprises small to medium-sized, ground-dwelling animals of around 1–2kg (2¼–4½lb), roughly half the eagle's own weight. In Britain this means mammals such as Rabbits and Mountain Hares, and birds such as Red Grouse and Ptarmigan. Staples elsewhere include ground squirrels in North America, marmots in the Alps and water birds in many areas.

To capture prey in open country, Golden Eagles use at least seven different hunting techniques (see page 57). These vary from soaring on high to spot prey, then descending upon it in a long attacking glide, to quartering low over the contours of a hillside and snatching prey flushed into the open. The technique varies with the target: to capture prey in flight, a Golden Eagle will stoop vertically at tremendous speed, like a Peregrine Falcon. To capture a large mammal, such as a young deer, it will latch on with its talons and 'ride' the unfortunate victim until it collapses.

The Golden Eagle is, in short, a powerful and very versatile hunter. Indeed, scientists have recorded more than 400 species in its diet worldwide, ranging from tiny

Below: The protective posture with which an eagle spreads its wings while feeding is known as 'mantling'.

songbirds to large mammals more than ten times its own weight (see page 53). The upper limit in prey size is more a reflection of carrying than killing power: a Golden Eagle struggles to lift anything heavier than itself, but is perfectly able to kill an adult deer.

This capacity for killing large mammals has led the Golden Eagle into serious trouble. Farmers around the world have long blamed the bird for taking their lambs and other livestock. In reality, such attacks are a very small part of the Golden Eagle's predatory behaviour in most of its range. In the UK, active predation on lambs is barely ever recorded. Eagles caught feeding on sheep carcasses are invariably taking advantages of dead animals they have come across: this raptor, whilst being a deadly hunter, is also a consummate scavenger.

Breeding and lifespan

Golden Eagles need lots of space in which to breed, with a range of up to 200km^2 (77 square miles) occupied by a single pair in some areas being among the largest of any bird. Individuals of both sexes mark their territory in spring, performing spectacular 'sky dance' display flights to repel competitors. Similar flights, in which both partners may drop then re-catch rocks and clods of earth, serve as courtship displays, to build and/or reaffirm pair bonds (see page 71).

Above: An elevated perch allows a Golden Eagle to scan for prey from a distance.

Golden Eagles usually mate for life. They often build their huge nests on inaccessible cliffs, where available, but in some parts of the world may also choose large, mature trees. A pair generally maintains several nests within a territory and may switch between them from one year to the next. The nests are constructed from heavy tree branches and lined with finer material. The pair adds to it each year and the massive resulting structure may exceed 2.5m (8ft) across and 5m (16ft) deep – although the norm is much less.

The female lays her eggs – usually two – in spring, and the eggs hatch after around 41–45 days of incubation, shared between the pair. The chicks – one or both – fledge after roughly 75 days, but stay with their parents for another three months or so as they learn to fly. Within a year they will usually have dispersed from the natal territory in order to make a life of their own.

Above: A cliff overhang offers a perfect, protected nest-site for a pair of Golden Eagles.

Life is tough for young Golden Eagles as they learn to fend for themselves. Many do not survive their first or second years. However, those that reach maturity start breeding from about five years and may live to more than 30 years in the wild. The challenges they face are legion. Natural predation is very rare – few other predators will even think of taking on an adult Golden Eagle – but humans pose numerous threats. These range from deliberate persecution (including by gamekeepers, farmers and egg collectors), to more insidious threats such as pesticides and the ongoing loss of habitat to agriculture and development.

Today the Golden Eagle is not considered threatened on a global scale, and is classed as Least Concern by the IUCN, with an estimated 60,000–100,000 breeding pairs worldwide. However, populations in many regions have declined steeply since the Industrial Revolution and continue to do so. In the UK this is an 'amber-listed' species – meaning that it has a low but stable population. Latest estimates suggest some 440 breeding pairs.

Golden or White-tailed?
ID tips for telling them apart

The two UK eagles may appear easy to tell apart in a book but things can be trickier in the field, where views are often distant and light poor. First, you must check that your eagle is not a buzzard. The latter is only about half as big (its wingspan is 30% smaller), but size can be hard to judge against a blank sky so focus on shape: eagles have proportionally longer wings, with clearer 'fingers', and a more protruding head and neck. Also, a buzzard never shows any white in its wings or tail. Then, once you are confident that your bird is an eagle, the following features will help you identify which species.

- **Shape**: a Golden Eagle's wings appear more elegant, with a curved trailing edge; a White-tailed Eagle's wings look massive and more rectangular; a White-tailed Eagle's head protrudes a little further; its tail is shorter and often fanned wide.
- **Flight pattern**: a flying White-tailed Eagle appears more ponderous and less dynamic than a Golden Eagle; a soaring Golden Eagle

often holds its wings in a shallow V whereas a White-tailed Eagle holds them flat. (A buzzard usually soars in tighter circles than either.)
- **Colour and markings**: an adult Golden Eagle appears all-dark apart from its golden nape (often hard to see); an adult White-tailed Eagle has a paler head and white tail; a young Golden Eagle has white wing patches and a white band across the tail; a White-tailed Eagle never has white in the wings; a perched White-tailed Eagle appears scruffier, and its huge yellow bill is more conspicuous.
- **Behaviour**: you will seldom see a White-tailed Eagle hunting inland, low over moorland or hillsides; you will *never* see a Golden Eagle diving into the sea; unlike White-tailed Eagles, Golden Eagles rarely perch on the ground, unless at a carcass.

Below: The Golden Eagle (left) has a slimmer, more elegant flight profile than the White-tailed Eagle (right).

Meet the White-tailed Eagle

The White-tailed Eagle (*Haliaeetus albicilla*) has a lower profile in the UK than the Golden Eagle. This may be partly because it disappeared from the country for much of the 20th century, before being reintroduced during the 1970s. However, there is no doubt that it has also failed to capture our imagination as a predator in quite the same way as the Golden Eagle, and has never enjoyed the same status as a cultural icon. It is perhaps surprising to some, then, that this magnificent raptor – also known as the Sea Eagle – is even larger than the Golden Eagle. In fact it is the UK's largest bird of prey and, just like its slightly smaller cousin, is a truly formidable predator.

Size and appearance

The White-tailed Eagle is a huge bird and, at 4–6.9kg/ 9–15lb (females) and 3.1–4.5kg/7–10lb (males), is on average slightly heavier than a Golden Eagle. Indeed, this species is on average the fourth largest eagle in the world. Its wingspan, at an average of 2.18m (7ft) – and exceptionally reaching 2.5m (8¼ft) – is the greatest on average of any eagle.

It is shape as well as size, however, that defines first impressions of this bird. For those previously only familiar with Golden Eagles, a first sighting of a White-tailed Eagle suggests a more massive but less dynamic bird. Its huge wings are broader, squarer and more vulture-like in shape, lacking the sculpted contours of its more elegant cousin. This impression is reinforced by its habit of holding them flat while gliding, rather than slightly upturned in the Golden Eagle's classic dihedral. Indeed, a flying White-

Below: The massive yellow bill of an adult White-tailed Eagle is even larger and more prominent than a Golden Eagle's.

tailed Eagle is often described as looking like a barn door or kitchen table. The flight silhouette also shows a head and neck that project further than a Golden Eagle's, but a tail that is shorter and forms a blunt wedge shape when fanned out – which it usually is.

Above: A White-tailed Eagle acquires its white tail only in full adult plumage, after about five years.

These features – the square wings, long neck and short, broad tail – are all typical of the *Haliaeetus* genus of eagles, commonly known as sea eagles. These birds are quite distinct from the *Aquila* genus, to which the Golden Eagle belongs, and are thought by some scientists to be closer in evolutionary heritage to the kites (*Milvus* genus). They are among the largest of all eagles and include among their ranks such other well-known species as the Bald Eagle of North America, the African Fish Eagle and the formidable Steller's Sea Eagle of the Russian far east – on average, the largest eagle in the world.

A closer look at the White-tailed Eagle reveals other features typical of this genus. Its massive yellow bill is even larger than that of a Golden Eagle and its bright yellow legs are unfeathered below the 'knee', though thickly scaled. As in other sea eagles, the head is strikingly pale – becoming almost creamy as the bird gets older – and adults have a pure white tail. Indeed, the tail can appear almost translucent when backlit by strong sunlight, making the bird appear tailless at a distance.

Otherwise the plumage appears more worn and unkempt than a Golden Eagle's, with pale feather edges on the upperparts producing a mottled, scalloped effect that increases with age. Perched on the ground, this bird can resemble a feathered haystack, with none of a Golden Eagle's gleaming sleekness. Immatures are darker, without a yellow bill or white tail. The white tail develops with age, showing more white each year until the bird reaches maturity, when it loses the black terminal band. Unlike in a Golden Eagle, however, the wings show no white at any age.

Where to see one

The White-tailed Eagle once ranged widely around the British coastline, but was systematically exterminated during the 19th century, finally disappearing in 1916. Today, following reintroduction in the 1970s to the

Below: The coast of north-west Scotland is the best place in Britain to see a White-tailed Eagle - if you're lucky, even catching a fish.

Isle of Mull (see page 119), it has re-established itself around the coast and islands of north-west Scotland and is slowly expanding its range. A separate population has also been reintroduced to the north-east Scottish coast and, more recently, to Ireland. White-tailed Eagles that occasionally turn up elsewhere in the British Isles are generally wanderers from mainland Europe.

Elsewhere, the White-tailed Eagle

occurs across northern mainland Europe and Asia, from Greenland in the west to Siberia and Japan in the east. Norway is home to much the largest European population, with up to 11,000 pairs. Isolated breeding populations occur in Greenland, Iceland and the Balkans. This species is largely sedentary, with only the very northernmost populations – such as those from northern Scandinavia and Siberia – migrating south in winter, some as far as the Arabian Gulf and South China Sea. Individuals from Siberia occasionally migrate across the Bering Straits to Alaska, and there is evidence that the bird once ranged as far south as Hawaii.

Above: The maps above show the White-tailed Eagle's worldwide range and (inset map) its range within Europe. Green shows where it is resident year-round; yellow shows where it is present only during the summer breeding season; blue shows where it is present only as a winter visitor.

A broad-brush world map shows that the range of the White-tailed Eagle overlaps in many areas with that of the Golden Eagle. Closer scrutiny at ground level, however, shows that the birds generally prefer different habitats, so are seldom found together. The White-tailed Eagle – as its alternative name, Sea Eagle, suggests – is a coastal bird throughout much of its range. Where it does occur inland, it is invariably around wetlands and water bodies. Forest is not an inhibiting factor to hunting, because this species takes most of its prey from the water. In fact, it generally nests in forest trees.

Food and hunting

Opposite: Despite its great size, the White-tailed Eagle is highly manoeuvrable in the air.

The White-tailed Eagle's choice of habitat, like that of the Golden Eagle, reflects its diet. It is a specialist at capturing aquatic prey. Fish are a favourite food, with a variety of marine and freshwater species on the menu, including commercial species snatched from fisheries and fish ponds. Water birds are also a staple in many areas, including seabirds such as Fulmars taken at their breeding colonies and waterfowl seized from lakes where they over-winter. Hunting White-tailed Eagles glide low over the water, hover for a moment, then drop down to snatch the prey in their talons. When hunting diving birds, they may make repeated passes at their target, which may duck down to escape but eventually return to the surface where, exhausted, they become easy quarry.

White-tailed Eagles are, however, highly versatile and opportunistic feeders, and take a wide variety of other live prey, including birds as big as swans and mammals up to the size of deer calves. Like other sea eagles they are adept pirates, stealing prey from other hunters. They also take a large amount of carrion – including deer, livestock and fish. In many areas carrion may become the primary food source, especially during winter, and birds may gather to share the feast. As is the case with the Golden Eagle, this bird's reputation as a killer of lambs and other livestock can largely be explained by its habit of scavenging on carcasses – and people leaping to the wrong conclusion. It is more than capable of killing a lamb, but this very seldom happens.

Breeding and lifespan

White-tailed Eagles occupy territories of 30–70km^2 (11–22 square miles), generally slightly smaller than those of Golden Eagles. They pair for life, becoming sexually mature at 4–5 years. A pair will renew its bond in a spectacular aerial courtship display, and this species is also much more vocal than the Golden Eagle, especially during the breeding season (see page 73).

A pair builds its massive stick nest in the crown of a tall tree or on a coastal cliff. The sticks used tend to be a little thicker than those favoured by Golden Eagles, and the nest may become even bigger; trees have been known to collapse under the weight of a nest. Successful nests are often reused and built up further every year. A female produces 1–3 eggs, laid 2–5 days apart in spring (in Scotland, March to early April). The parents take turns at incubation and the eggs hatch after 38 days. The first hatchling is generally larger and stronger than its siblings, but the youngsters are reasonably tolerant of each other and – unlike in Golden Eagles – siblicide seldom occurs in this species. The young can feed themselves at 5–6 weeks and fledge at 11–12

Above: An immature White-tailed Eagle waits on the ice; surviving its first winter will be a challenge.

weeks. They will hang around the nest, dependent upon their parents, for up to ten more weeks, before heading out to fend for themselves (see also page 82).

Like Golden Eagles, young White-tailed Eagles are vulnerable in their early years, and must rely a great deal on scavenging as their hunting skills continue to develop. If they can get through their first winter, their survival chances increase. They fear very few natural predators, and may reach the age of 25 or more. Their greatest threats come from our species. These include poisoning from pesticides and other environmental pollutants, which work their way up the food chain through bioaccumulation, direct persecution from those who consider the raptors (usually wrongly) a threat to their livestock, and collision with obstacles such as wind turbines.

The White-tailed Eagle population plummeted across much of Europe during the period 1800–1970, but has been recovering since the 1980s with the help of some

far-sighted conservation and reintroduction programmes. Today this species is classed as of Least Concern by the IUCN. However, its worldwide population is much smaller than that of the Golden Eagle, with an estimated 20,300–39,600 mature individuals worldwide. In the UK it remains on the Red List, as the newly reintroduced population continues slowly to establish itself. In 2015 the UK breeding population reached 100 pairs for the first time.

Above: White-tailed Eagles commonly nest in large trees.

Ancestors and Relatives

The White-tailed Eagle and Golden Eagle are among up to 71 bird species around the world that go by the name 'eagle'. The precise number depends upon which authority you follow, with recent advances in DNA-based taxonomy having caused major readjustments in the traditional classification of birds, including eagles. The science remains contentious and is not the concern of this book. Nonetheless, it helps us to better understand our two species if we know something about where they came from, and how they fit today into the great filing cabinet of the world's raptors.

Eagle origins

First things first: eagles are birds. Even the most radical taxonomist has not yet disputed that. And birds, as most schoolchildren now know, evolved from dinosaurs – probably from the small, fast-running theropod group, which initially developed feathers as a form of insulation before evolution subsequently harnessed their potential for flight. The oldest known bird is the celebrated *Archaeopteryx*, a crow-sized creature that retained many reptilian traits, including teeth and tailbones, and which inhabited central Europe during the Jurassic Period some 150 million years ago. Birds proliferated during the Cretaceous Period that followed, diversifying into many families and staking their claims to environmental niches from forests to oceans.

Above: A fossil of *Archaeopteryx*, an ancestor of birds from the Jurassic Period.

The earliest known birds of prey date back some 50 million years to the Eocene Epoch, and were the ancestors of today's kites (*Milvus* genus). They were primarily scavengers, which preyed on dead fish in coastal and wetland areas. The first eagles were descended from this line and were the forerunners of today's sea eagles, such as our White-tailed Eagle, with

Left: The Martial Eagle is the largest eagle in Africa and commonly preys on guineafowl.

Above: The Red Kite is descended from the same early raptor ancestors as the White-tailed Eagle's.

the earliest known species dating back some 36 million years. Like the kites, they had unfeathered lower legs, with sharp talons and tiny spines – called spicules – on their feet to give them a firmer grip on their slippery prey.

From these early roots, eagles diversified into a multiplicity of forms, including the 'booted' eagles, with their fully feathered legs, which were the forerunners of today's Golden Eagle. Predatory adaptations evolved thick and fast as the planet's ever-changing environments continued to open up new ecological niches. Species came and went along the way, and included some truly fearsome birds. In recent history none was more impressive than Haast's Eagle (*Harpagornis moorei*). This 15kg (22lb) giant, descended from much smaller booted eagles, inhabited the South Island of New Zealand, where it preyed on moas – huge, flightless, ostrich-like birds that could weigh more than ten times their attacker. They eventually died out in around 1400, after the Maori arrived and hunted out this source of food.

Eagle giant

The extinct Haast's Eagle (*Harpagornis moorei*) was probably the largest eagle that ever took to the skies. A female weighed 10–15kg and measured up to 140cm long, some 40% larger than the biggest eagles today. Its massive 11cm bill dwarfed that of Steller's Sea Eagle, whose 7cm bill is the largest among modern eagles.

This formidable raptor inhabited the South Island of New Zealand, where it hunted moas – huge, flightless, ostrich-like birds that were up to 15 times heavier. It is thought to have attacked in a high-speed dive, grasping the moa's pelvis with one foot and striking at its head or neck with the other. Its relatively short wings (at 2.5m, its wingspan was little bigger than a White-tailed Eagle's) can be explained by the fact that, like a Harpy Eagle (see page 40), it needed to manoeuvre rapidly through dense cover in pursuit of its prey.

Below: Haast's Eagle was the largest predator ever known on the New Zealand mainland.

DNA studies suggest that Haast's Eagle was descended from today's Booted Eagle (*Hieraaetus pennatus*) and Little Eagle (*Hieraaetus morphnoides*), which weigh just 600– 800g. This spectacular increase in size was probably a predatory adaptation that reflected both the large size of its prey and the absence of any competition. Indeed, with no terrestrial mammals or other large predators on New Zealand, Haast's Eagle would have had its kills all to itself.

The Maori, who arrived in around 1280, brought about the demise of Haast's Eagle by hunting out the moas on which it subsisted. By 1400 the giant raptor had followed its prey to extinction. To this day, however, it features as the *Pouakai* of Maori legend – even, in some traditional stories, preying on humans. Given its size and power, this might not have been beyond the bounds of possibility.

Eagles in order

Above: The Osprey belongs to a different family from eagles, the Pandionidae, of which it is the only member.

Today's eagles belong to the Accipitridae. This is one of three families that constitute the Accipitriformes – in turn, one of some 28 recognised bird orders extant today. It embraces the vast majority of birds of prey, including hawks, kites, harriers, buzzards and Old World vultures, with species ranging in size from the dinky 85g (3oz) Little Sparrowhawk (*Accipiter minullus*) to the huge 14kg (31lb) Cinereous Vulture (*Aegypius monachus*). The two other families in this order each contain just a single species: the Pandionidae is represented by the Osprey (*Pandion haliaetus*); the Sagittariidae by the Secretary Bird (*Sagittarius serpentarius*).

You may wonder why falcons, such as the Peregrine Falcon (*Falco peregrinus*), are absent from the Accipitridae line-up. Although traditionally classified as birds of prey, recent research has revealed that these predatory birds have closer evolutionary affinities with parrots. Their physical similarity to hawks and other raptors reflects a process called convergent evolution, through which different groups of animals, often in different parts of the world, evolve similar characteristics in response to sharing the same environmental challenges (in this case hunting and killing). Indeed, scientists now assign falcons their own order (Falconiformes), as they do for New World vultures (Cathatiformes).

But back to eagles: the 71 or so species recognised today fall into up to 23 genera – again, according to whom you believe. The evolutionary affinities of these birds remain an object of ongoing study, with some former 'races' now having been assigned full species status, and others having been moved from one genus to another as DNA studies clarify their genetic relationships. Bonelli's Eagle (*Aquila fasciata*), for instance, has been moved from the genus *Hieraaetus* to *Aquila*, so is thus now closer to the Golden Eagle.

These taxonomic waters can appear very muddy. However, for everyday purposes it is still possible to divide up today's eagles into four basic groups, each of which can be identified by similarities in the appearance and behaviour of its members. They are as follows:

Sea eagles
(also known as fish eagles)
Large to very large eagles that are closely related to kites, from which they originally descended. All have broad, vulture-like wings, a huge yellow bill, and a pale or white head and/or tail. The White-tailed Eagle belongs in this group. Others include the American Bald Eagle (*Haliaeetus leucocephalus*), African Fish Eagle (*H. vocifer*) and Steller's Sea Eagle (*H. pelagicus*), the last of these being the biggest of all eagles. Some authorities also include the Palmnut Vulture (*Gypohierax angolensis*), an African species that lives largely on palm nuts and is thus a uniquely vegetarian raptor. Sea eagles inhabit coastal or aquatic habitats, with most species feeding on fish and carrion. Many are kleptoparasites – pirating prey from other predators.

Above: The White-bellied Sea Eagle, found around the coast of Australia and South East Asia, is a close relative of the White-tailed Eagle.

Above: The Tawny Eagle is a common *Aquila* species of African savannahs.

Above: The Black-breasted Snake Eagle is an African species of open country, where it scans from an elevated perch for reptilian prey.

Booted eagles

(also known as 'true' eagles)
The largest group of eagles, with more than 30 species in some ten genera, including *Aquila*, of which the Golden Eagle is a member. They range in size from the 750g (26oz) Booted Eagle (*Hieraatus pennatus*), to huge predators such as the Martial Eagle (*Polemaetus bellicosus*) of Africa. All genera have feathered legs down to the toes (hence 'booted'), and many are known for their dynamic flight and rapacious predatory behaviour, often taking prey larger than themselves.

Snake eagles

Small to medium-sized eagles confined largely to tropical Africa and Asia, where they are adapted to hunting reptiles. Key features include unfeathered lower legs, a conspicuously large head and big, powerful eyes adapted to spotting prey from a distance. Most scan for their prey from a high perch or while hovering, then drop to capture it on the ground. Six genera are represented, including *Circaetus*, comprising the snake eagles of Africa, and *Spilornis*, comprising the serpent eagles of tropical Asia. An unusual member of this group is the Bateleur Eagle (*Terathopius ecaudatus*) of African savannahs, which spends much of its time airborne and scavenges like a vulture (see page 39).

Forest eagles

A small group of large, powerful eagles adapted for hunting in tropical forests, with relatively short wings to enable easier flight among trees. Includes the huge Harpy Eagle (*Harpia harpyja*) of tropical South America, which has the largest talons of any raptor and preys upon sloths, monkeys and other forest-canopy mammals. The critically endangered Philippine Eagle (*Pithecophaga jefferyi*) shares many characteristics of this group, as does the African Crowned Eagle (*Stephanoaetus coronatus*), both being very large, powerful eagles adapted to canopy hunting. Taxonomists, however, now group the former with the snake eagles and the latter with the booted eagles, with each thought to have acquired its adaptive traits through convergent evolution.

Above: The Philippine Eagle, formerly known as Monkey-eating Eagle, is one of the most powerful of all species.

Classification of UK eagles

Still following? Assuming you are, you will have grasped that our two species of eagle fall into two very different genera. The Golden Eagle belongs to the *Aquila* genus of booted or 'true' eagles. The White-tailed Eagle belongs to the *Haliaeetus* genus of sea eagles. This is how the two species line up in a taxonomic table.

Kingdom	Animalia (animals)
Phylum	Chordata (vertebrates)
Class	Aves (birds)
Order	Accipitriformes (diurnal birds of prey)
Family	Accipitridae (eagles, hawks, buzzards)
Genus	*Aquila* (booted eagles) and *Haliaeetus* (sea eagles)
Species	*Aquila chrysaetos* (Golden Eagle), *Haliaeetus ablicilla* (White-tailed Eagle)

Races and subspecies

It gets even more complicated. Below the level of species there is yet one more rung on the taxonomic ladder. Known as 'subspecies', or sometimes 'race', this applies to the slightly different forms of a single species that have evolved as different populations of that species have become geographically – and so genetically – isolated from one another in different parts of the world. In the language of classification, a subspecies is recognised with a trinomial, or three-part scientific name. Thus, for example, the scientific name for the Sumatran Tiger is *Panthera tigris sumatrae*. This breaks down as: genus, big cats *(Panthera)*; species, tiger *(tigris)*; and subspecies Sumatran *(sumatrae)*.

The White-tailed Eagle does not have any recognised subspecies; in other words, all White-tailed Eagles around the world are pretty much the same. Some scientists have proposed subspecies status for the Greenland population, based on the consistently large size of these birds, but genetic evidence does not back this up.

In the case of the Golden Eagle, things are not so simple. Scientists today recognise up to six separate subspecies of this bird, as follows:

Below: Golden Eagles in the UK belong to the European subspecies, which is the nominate race.

Aquila chrysaetos chrysaetos
(European Golden Eagle)
This is the nominate subspecies – in other words, the race by which the species was first named. It occurs across much of northern and western Europe, including Scotland, Scandinavia, France, Italy and Austria; in Eastern Europe from Estonia and Russia south to Greece and Bulgaria; and as far east as western Kazakhstan and northern Iran. This is a medium-sized race: males average 3.69kg (8lb) and females 5.17kg (11½lb). It is also the palest, with tawny golden-brown upperparts and a gleaming golden, long-feathered nape-patch.

Aquila chrysaetos homeyeri
(Iberian/Arabian Golden Eagle)
This race occurs in almost the whole Iberian Peninsula, as well as in Crete. Outside Europe it ranges across Asia Minor, from Turkey through the Arabian Peninsula to the Caucasus and western Iran. It is slightly smaller and darker than the nominate race, but not as dark as birds found further east. It has a dark brownish forehead and crown, with the nape-patch being short-feathered and a light rusty colour.

Above: The Iberian or Arabian Golden Eagle inhabits largely arid country and is a little smaller than Golden Eagles found in the UK.

Aquila chrysaetos daphanea
(Asian/Himalayan Golden Eagle)
This race ranges from central Kazakhstan, eastern Iran and the easternmost Caucasus east to Manchuria and central China; and along the Himalayas from northern Pakistan east to Bhutan and north-eastern Myanmar. It is the largest race on average, with males weighing around 4.05kg (9lb) and females 6.35kg (14lb) – the latter being roughly the same as a King Charles Spaniel – and a wingspan averaging 2.21m (7¼ft). It is also generally the second darkest, with a blackish back, dark forehead and crown, and rich red-brown nape. Also known as the Berkut, the Himalayan Golden Eagle was the first race to be used in falconry – a practice that continues to this day on the steppes of Mongolia and Kazakhstan (see page 110).

Above: The Himalayan Golden Eagle of central Asia, also known as the Berkut, is the largest race.

Above: The Japanese race is much the smallest and darkest of Golden Eagle subspecies.

Aquila chrysaetos japonica
(Japanese Golden Eagle)
This race is found in northern Japan and undefined parts of Korea. It is much the smallest race, with males weighing approximately 2.5kg (5½lb) and females 3.25kg (7lb). It is also the darkest, with adults being a slaty-black on the back and crown. The bright rufous nape feathers are quite loose and long. Adults often have white mottling on the tail that is more typical of juveniles in other races.

Aquila chrysaetos kamtschatica
(Siberian/Kamchatka Golden Eagle)
This race ranges from Western Siberia, where it may overlap with the nominate race, across most of Russia (spilling over into Northern Mongolia) to the Kamchatka Peninsula and Anadyrsky District. It has roughly the same colouration as the American Golden Eagle, and indeed some authorities consider it to be the same race. However, it is much larger, being nearly the equal of the Asian Golden Eagle in average wing length.

Aquila chrysaetos canadensis
(American Golden Eagle)
This is the only race found in North America, and is the most wide-ranging of all. It occurs across most of Alaska, western Canada and the western United States, and south to central Mexico, although it is now extinct as a breeding species in the eastern United States. A medium-sized race, males average 3.48kg (7½lb) in weight and females 4.91kg (11lb). The plumage is blackish to dark brown on the back, with long, rusty-red nape feathers that are slightly narrower and darker than in the nominate race. With an estimated population of 50,000–70,000 breeding pairs, the American Golden Eagle is much the most numerous race of this species.

Within each race of Golden Eagle there is individual variation, with weights of over 7kg (15½lb) and wingspans topping 2.5m (8ft) recorded for exceptional wild birds. Even larger measurements have been recorded from some birds raised in captivity.

Above: The American Golden Eagle is the most numerous of all Golden Eagle subspecies.

A world of eagles

Eagles are found on every continent except Antarctica, and have adapted to every habitat from desert and mountaintop to tropical rainforest and sea cliffs. The sheer range of species and the variety of lifestyles they embrace is testimony to the great success of these ultimate avian predators. The following are just a few examples.

Above: The African Fish Eagle inhabits inland rivers and waterways across sub-Saharan Africa.

African Fish Eagle (*Haliaeetus vocifer*)
The ringing cry of this striking bird is routinely described as the 'voice of Africa'. One of the smaller sea eagles, with females measuring up to 75cm (30in), it is nonetheless perhaps the noisiest and most conspicuous, with its snow-white head and tail and impressive dives for fish. The famous call, a gull-like *kyow yow-yow*, is uttered with the head thrown back, often in duet with a mate. Prey is mostly fish, plucked from the water's surface with outstretched talons, following a long, slanting dive. Like other sea eagles, this species will also rob other animals of their catch, and sometimes hunts waterfowl – including even flamingoes. It breeds on large lakes and rivers across sub-Saharan Africa.

Bateleur Eagle (*Terathopius ecaudatus*)
This medium-sized raptor is one of the more curious birds to take the name eagle. A distinctive sight above the African savannah, it derives its name from the French for 'tightrope walker' – a reference to its tilting motion in flight – and with its long, narrow-tipped wings cuts an unmistakable dash in the air. The short tail, big head and (in adults) colourful patchwork plumage further help distinguish it from other raptors. Although widespread, Bateleurs are common only in protected areas, particularly big-game parks. They frequently take carrion and their low-level flight often makes them the first scavenger at a carcass, sometimes providing a clue to the location of a treed Leopard kill.

Above: When perched, the tips of a Bateleur's long wings extend well beyond its short tail.

Booted Eagle (*Aquila pennata*)
This buzzard-sized raptor is one of the smallest eagles, with large females weighing no more than 1kg (2¼lb). Despite its diminutive size, it belongs to the same *Aquila* genus as the Golden Eagle and is one of the closest living relatives of New Zealand's enormous extinct Haast's Eagle (see page 29). This species inhabits hilly, wooded country from the Mediterranean and North Africa east across much of Asia, and migrates in large numbers to winter in sub-Saharan Africa and South Asia. A bold and dynamic hunter, it captures prey with a dramatic falcon-like stoop, and may take birds many times its own size. Two colour morphs occur: a light one and a dark one.

Above: Look out for Booted Eagles when on summer holiday in Spain or southern France.

Above: Like many eagles, the Crested Serpent Eagle erects its crest when alarmed in order to appear more intimidating.

Above: The Harpy Eagle is the apex predator of the Amazon rainforest tree canopy, feeding on sloths and monkeys.

Crested Serpent Eagle (*Spilornis cheela*)
This medium-sized eagle is widespread across tropical Asia, from India to Borneo. Several isolated island forms – including the Andaman and South Nicobar Serpent Eagles – are now considered species in their own right. It is a stocky-looking bird, with a bare yellow face and a mane of long feathers that creates a thick-necked appearance. As in all specialist snake-eating raptors, its bare legs are thickly scaled for protection against the snakes and other reptiles that make up its staple diet. A bird of wooded hillsides and forests, it is usually seen soaring over the canopy – where the broad white bands on its wings and tail are conspicuous – or perched in a tree top, often attracting attention with a piercing three-note call.

Harpy Eagle (*Harpia harpyja*)
This formidable raptor is the largest eagle of the Americas and, with females weighing up to 9kg (20lb), one of the two heaviest in the world on average. It inhabits dense lowland rainforest in the Amazon basin – ranging as far north as Costa Rica – and is the apex predator of the forest canopy, capturing prey such as sloths and monkeys that may weigh as much as itself. It has relatively short wings for its size, to aid manoeuvrability through the branches, but its talons – with a hind claw that, up to 13cm (6in), is longer than a Grizzly Bear's – are the largest and most powerful of any raptor. Harpy Eagles generally hunt by sitting silently in the canopy to spot prey below, but may also soar above the trees and will also pursue and capture macaws and other birds in flight. Despite its wide range, this bird has declined heavily due to habitat loss and persecution, and is classed as Near Threatened by the IUCN.

Verreaux's Eagle (*Aquila verreauxii*)
This striking eagle, up to 90cm (35in) in length, is a close relative of the Golden Eagle. It occurs in rocky and mountainous regions across sub-Saharan Africa, with a few scattered outposts in the Arabian Peninsula. Very similar to the Golden Eagle in size and ecology, it differs by its jet-black plumage, emblazoned with bold white markings. Pairs stick close together and often hunt in tandem, gliding low over rocky hillsides in search of hyraxes – their staple diet. This species has been studied intensively in the Matobo Hills of Zimbabwe, where there is an unusually high density.

Above: The black-and-white plumage and distinctive narrow base to the wings make the Verreaux's Eagle unmistakable.

Wedge-tailed Eagle (*Aquila audax*)
The third largest of eagles by average length (95cm/37in) and average wingspan (210cm/83in), this is the largest bird of prey in Australia. Indeed, the 284cm (112in) wingspan of one Tasmanian individual remains the record for any eagle. It is similar to the Golden Eagle in general appearance, but slighter in build, with a longer and distinctively diamond-shaped tail that creates an unmistakable flight silhouette. This species preys on mammals, both native (such as wallabies) and invasive (such as Rabbits), as well as large reptiles and birds. It readily takes carrion and is often seen scavenging from roadkill in the outback, unfortunately sometimes itself falling victim to traffic in the process.

Above: Look out beside the highway when crossing Australia's outback, where Wedge-tailed Eagles often descend to prey on roadkill.

A View to a Kill

Let's not beat about the bush: eagles are killers. These birds depend for their survival upon their ability to do other animals in – and the two British species, both being exceptionally large and well armed, are among the most formidable predators on the planet. They occupy the apex predator niche wherever they occur, on a par with the likes of wolves. But killing is not always easy, even for an eagle. Prey is hard to capture and it takes years of trial-and-error experience to learn the arts, with the price of failure being death by starvation. Luckily there is more than one way to grab a bite and these 'proud' birds, as we like to depict them, are not above scavenging an old carcass or even stealing someone else's catch.

Fit for purpose

One glance at an eagle – Golden or White-tailed – and you know it is a predator. Even without the hooked beak and talons, the forwards-facing eyes and phenomenal powers of flight reveal that this is a bird built for focusing upon and pursuing a target. Each part of its anatomy has evolved to make this job easier.

Talons

A Golden Eagle's talons are among the most lethal weapons in the animal kingdom. Each foot is about the size of a human hand and has four toes, three facing forwards and one backwards, each ending in a wickedly sharp claw. The hallux, or hind claw, is the longest and measures 4.5–6cm (1¾–2¼in). Together, these fearsome digits can exert a crushing force of 200kg (440lb) per 6.45cm² (1 square inch). To put this into simple terms, we are talking about a bird that weighs no more than a house cat but has claws longer than a Tiger's and a grip at least ten times stronger than our own – indeed, more powerful than the bite of a pit bull.

Above: The talons of a Golden Eagle are longer than a tiger's claws.

Left: A Golden Eagle prepares to tear into the carcass of a Roe Deer.

Above: A hunting Golden Eagle extends its talons when striking prey.

The talons do several jobs. The first is to kill the prey. They achieve this by crushing its skull or piercing its vital organs, the claws being driven in like blades right to the hilt. With smaller prey, death is almost instantaneous. With larger prey, such as ungulates, it may take longer, the victim eventually collapsing through blood loss, internal damage and exhaustion as the eagle hangs on.

This process of 'hanging on' – of getting and maintaining a grip – is the talons' other main task. The eagle must secure its hold until the prey is dead, both to prevent it from escaping and also to keep it at arm's length so that it does not cause any damage in its struggle to escape. Once the prey is dead, the talons must pin down the carcass while the eagle pulls strenuously to pluck or dismember it. And they must cling on tight as the eagle takes off and carries the prey away to its eyrie – or to a more secure, elevated perch.

A White-tailed Eagle's talons are not quite as powerful as a Golden Eagle's, as it relies a little less on killing large, potentially dangerous prey. However, its unfeathered lower legs and toes are coated with spiny scales, called spicules, that offer a better purchase on slippery, struggling fish. The Osprey, another fish-eating raptor, has a similar adaptation.

An eagle's talons are also formidable weapons in self-defence. The long legs enable it to strike vicious blows at some distance from its body – either when battling with others of its own kind over a carcass, or when defending itself against an attacker. An eagle surprised on the ground will fall on its back and strike upwards with its talons towards the head of its assailant.

Bill

The hooked bill of a bird of prey has evolved not so much for killing prey as for butchering the carcass afterwards. Falcons are the exception in that they use a small notch in the bill – the tomial tooth – to kill their catch. However, falcons are no longer thought to be closely related to eagles, hawks and other typical raptors, and are today placed in their own order: the Falconiformes (see page 30).

Below: A White-tailed Eagle tears at a carcass with its powerful bill.

Eagles have proportionally larger bills than all other raptors except the very largest vultures. Of the two UK species, a White-tailed Eagle's bill is the larger: this bright yellow, hatchet-like appendage measures up to 6.5cm (2½in) along the culmen (the ridgeline of the upper mandible) and is almost as long as the bird's head. The Golden Eagle's bill is a little smaller, with an average culmen length of 4.5cm (1¾in), and although the cere (the skin at the base of the bill) is yellow, the bill itself is horn coloured, with a black tip.

An eagle uses its bill primarily as a feeding tool.

Plucking and tearing with the hooked tip, and gouging with the sharp, blade-like edges, it is able to extract every last scrap of meat from a carcass. The bill is made of keratin – the same substance from which fingernails and horns are formed – and keeps growing throughout an eagle's lifetime in order to counter wear and tear.

Above: The eye of a Golden Eagle is larger than ours and provides eyesight up to eight times as powerful.

Eyes

Eagles have among the strongest eyesight in the animal kingdom. Studies suggest it is 4–8 times stronger than that of the average human and enables them to spot a rabbit from 3km (2 miles) away. Both UK species have eyes of around 4.5cm (1¾in) diameter – larger than ours. Like those of all predators, they are set on the front of the head and can focus both sideways and forwards. The latter allows stereoscopic vision, which is vital for the depth perception that a swooping eagle requires for an accurate strike. As the bird descends, its eye muscles continuously adjust the curvature of the eyeballs to maintain sharp focus. The large eyeballs fit so tightly into their sockets, however, that the eagle generally turns its head rather than its eyes to adjust its view, rotating it by up to 270 degrees, while sitting or flying.

The very large pupils of an eagle's eyes maximise the amount of light that reaches the retina, where the fovea – the most light-sensitive part – has a million light-sensitive cells per square millimetre, compared with just 200,000 in humans. This allows exceptional resolution, clarity and colour vision. While our eyes can see just three basic colours, eagles see five, and can thus distinguish well-camouflaged prey from its background at a great distance.

Eagles blink upwards, as their top eyelid is larger than the bottom one. Behind these two eyelids is a third transparent one, the nictitating membrane, which sweeps like a windscreen wiper across the eye to keep it clean. The fierce, penetrating expression of an eagle's eyes comes from the prominent brow ridge, which helps protect the eyes from the claws of struggling prey.

Above: Taking off from the ground requires maximum muscular effort for a Golden Eagle.

Wings

Above: A White-tailed Eagle spreads its wings and tail in order to brake and change direction suddenly.

Eagles are wonderful flyers, able to soar high to spot prey, glide vast distances without expending energy on flapping and plunge down at lightning speed on their quarry. Their low 'wing loading' – the ratio of body weight to wing-surface area – maximises their ability to gain lift from thermals and updraft. By soaring on outstretched wings, an eagle can gain height without flapping. And by folding its wings back a little and closing the slots between the long, tapered primaries (or 'fingers'), it can turn this upwards spiral into a long and extremely rapid horizontal glide. A Golden Eagle may reach speeds of up to 190km/h (118mph) when gliding in this way – and by folding its wings right back against its body and steepening the angle of descent, it can accelerate into a controlled dive, stooping like an outsized Peregrine Falcon at speeds of 240–320km/h (150–200mph). The sudden braking of the bird by spreading its wings at the point of impact can create a tearing sound audible for some distance. 'Like a thunderbolt it falls,' said Tennyson, and he was not far wrong.

The White-tailed Eagle is not as fast or dynamic in the air as the Golden Eagle, but its even longer and broader wings allow it even greater lift. Indeed, its glide ratio (speed of forwards travel divided by speed of descent) of up to 15:1 is among the highest of any British bird. Moreover, for a bird of such size it is capable of great speed, control and agility. This is especially impressive when diving on prey in the water, dodging harassment from smaller birds and tumbling through the air in its spectacular courtship display.

Both eagles appear at their most cumbersome when taking flight from the ground or a low perch. Flapping flight demands huge amounts of energy for birds their size, and they must flap heavily in order to gain lift and momentum. These flaps, however, illustrate the birds' great power, enabling them to lift prey that weighs as much as they do and carry it over several kilometres to an eyrie. Typically, they flap in bursts of 6–8 deep wingbeats, interspersed with two- to three-second glides.

Above: By folding backs its wings a Golden Eagle may accelerate from a fast glide into a rapid stoop on prey.

Prey

Both UK eagles take a wide variety of food, with everything from frogs to foxes falling victim to those lethal talons. Neither bird is fussy: the main goal is to satisfy its daily nutritional requirements and, during the breeding season, those of its chicks, and it will take anything available towards that end. In any given area, however, it is generally a handful of species – those that are most

Above: White-tailed Eagles take a large proportion of carrion in their diet, especially during winter.

easily available and that provide the greatest nutritional reward for the energy expended on their capture – that make up the bulk of the diet for both birds.

The two eagles seldom compete over food, as each is adapted to hunt in a different way and their preferences seldom coincide. For each species, the size limit of prey reflects more what the bird can carry than what it can kill. The Golden Eagle in particular can kill animals many times its own size and occasionally does so. However, being unable to carry anything much heavier than themselves, both birds tend to stick to prey within that limit. That is, unless they are feeding on a large carcass – which generally happens outside the breeding season, when there is no need to carry food back to the eyrie.

The Golden Eagle menu

A Golden Eagle needs on average 230–250g (8–9oz) of food per day, although it may go without for a week or gorge on up to 900g (32oz) at one sitting. The shyness of this bird and the remoteness of its habitat make its predatory behaviour hard to study. Much of what we know about its diet comes from analysis of prey remains found at the nest, or coughed up in pellets (see page 54). Inevitably, many food items are taken without any evidence being left behind.

Hundreds of different animal species are prey for Golden Eagles across the world. These range from rodents weighing no more than 10g (½oz) to small ungulates such as fawns and wild goats that may, exceptionally, weigh more than 30kg (88lb). Despite such variety, however, studies have discovered that the average breeding pair subsists on just 3.57 prey species, and that the average weight of prey is 1.6kg (3½lb) – typically consisting of mammals such as rabbits and game birds such as Ptarmigan.

Preferences vary by region: Golden Eagles in Mongolia, for instance, take a higher proportion of larger prey, with 15 per cent of their catches weighing more than 4kg (9lb). The menu also reflects the season and the age of the eagle. Many records of predation on larger mammals involve younger eagles and are during winter. These birds have no need to transport food to the nest, so may kill prey they cannot carry; and winter weather may leave larger prey in poor condition – so more vulnerable to attack – and smaller prey harder to find.

Above: A Golden Eagle in Norway plucks a Willow Grouse it has captured. Medium-sized game birds are among the most important prey for this raptor throughout its range.

Above: A Golden Eagle feeds on an Arctic Hare.

Above: Displaying Capercaillie.

Above: Arctic Ground Squirrel.

The Golden Eagle's worldwide menu falls into the following broad categories:

Rabbits and hares (*leporids*) These medium-sized mammals are the staple diet in many regions and make up some 32 per cent of the menu worldwide. Species taken include (in Scotland) the Mountain Hare and European Rabbit and (in the United States) the Jackrabbit. They are generally caught while foraging in the open. A large hare may be dismembered before it is carried back to the nest.

Game birds These plump, ground-dwelling birds are the dominant avian item on the eagle menu and make up some 10.3 per cent of its diet worldwide. Typical birds are grouse such as the Ptarmigan and Red Grouse (Scotland and Scandinavia), but also included are pheasants, partridges and such huge birds as the Wild Turkey (United States) and Capercaillie. Eagles generally capture game birds on the ground or just above it as they take off in a bid to escape. Male Capercaillies, which can weigh as much as an eagle, are vulnerable during their lek (territorial display), when they become heedless of danger. This would be an exceptionally unusual occurrence in Scotland, where Capercaillies are very rare, but has been recorded regularly in Scandinavia.

Ground squirrels These stocky colonial rodents comprise species such as the Alpine Marmot (in the Alps) and Prairie Dog (American prairies). They are the staple diet in most regions where leporids are absent, and make up some 12 per cent of the Golden Eagle's menu worldwide. The challenge for the eagle is to take them by surprise before they dash down their burrows.

Ungulates This is the most controversial section of the Golden Eagle menu because, in addition to wild animals such as deer, it may occasionally extend to livestock (see page 126). Golden Eagles are certainly capable of killing mammals many times their own size. The flesh of large mammals, however, makes up a small proportion of their diet and generally comes from carrion – animals already dead that the eagle scavenges. Predation on live ungulates is rare and generally opportunistic. The prey is both difficult and dangerous to kill (a Golden Eagle has been recorded killed by a Red Deer hind defending its calf), and impossible to transport to the nest. It is usually young animals that fall victim. These range from Reindeer in Scandinavia to Chamois in the Alps and Saiga in Mongolia. Remarkable recent camera-trap footage from Russia shows a young Sika Deer of some 25–30kg (55–66lb) attacked and killed by a Golden Eagle. In such attacks the eagle generally strikes from behind, targeting the skull or vital organs and riding the prey until it collapses. In mountainous areas it may also deliberately drive or pull a young animal – such as a Chamois or ibex – over a precipice to its death on the rocks below, then descend to feed on the carcass.

Above: A Golden Eagle scavenging on a Roe Deer.

Other mammals A Golden Eagle will grab anything furry that it thinks it can tackle. In Scotland this bird is the only regular predator of the Red Fox, and in Mongolia the smaller Corsac Fox makes up a significant part of its diet. The young of larger carnivores are not exempt, and records exist of Golden Eagles taking baby badgers, otters, Bobcats, Wolverines and even bear cubs. A 13.5kg (30lb) adult Coyote has been killed in the United States, and hunters' eagles in Mongolia (see page 108) are even flown at Wolves – which, although a small local race, are nonetheless daunting adversaries. At the other end of the scale, Golden Eagles will take rats, voles and numerous other small rodents.

Above: Red Foxes occasionally fall prey to Golden Eagles, although adults are formidable adversaries.

Other birds At least 200 bird species around the world are known to have ended up inside a Golden Eagle. As well as game birds (see above), common targets include crows, waterfowl and large waders such as Curlews. Victims range in size from a 10g (½oz) Meadow Pipit to a 10kg (22lb) Mute Swan. Other raptors are not immune, although they are often attacked more as competitors than as food, and in some places Golden Eagles target large migrating birds,

Above: A Golden Eagle feeding on a Rock Ptarmigan.

attacking Demoiselle Cranes over the Himalayas, for example, and knocking them from the air just as a Peregrine Falcon would a pigeon.

Unusual prey Golden Eagles are nothing if not versatile. They have been observed hunting frogs in an upland bog and scavenging fish from a frozen lake. In some areas they have developed very specific preferences. On the Swedish island of Gotland, for example, Hedgehogs make up 42 per cent of the local Golden Eagles' diet, while in parts of south-east Europe this species takes a significant number of tortoises. In the case of the latter, the eagles have learned to drop the armoured reptiles from a height onto rocks below in order to smash open the shell. Indeed, the Greek playwright Aeschylus (c. 525/524 – c. 456/455 BC) reputedly met his fate when a tumbling tortoise struck him on the head. Ironically, according to Pliny the historian, the great tragedian had been staying outdoors at the time in order to avoid the fulfilment of a prophecy that he would be killed by a falling object.

Above: Tortoises feature on the Golden Eagle menu in Mediterranean regions.

Coughing up the truth

One way in which eagles reveal what they have been eating is through the pellets that they cough up. These consist of the indigestible parts of their meals, such as fur, hair, bones and feathers, which gather in a bird's gizzard – the muscular part of its stomach where food is broken down – and are regurgitated through its mouth. Unlike the pellets of owls, eagle pellets contain few bones. This is because eagles do not swallow their food whole, as owls do, but use their bills to tear the flesh from their prey. An eagle's pellets are generally found in one of its regular resting or roosting places. They are much larger than owl pellets – up to 12cm (5in) in length. Scientists can break down a pellet, and by identifying its components – sometimes via DNA analysis – can determine what the bird has been eating.

Above: White-tailed Eagle pellets

How Golden Eagles hunt

Golden Eagles are daylight hunters that tend to go about their task in wide, open spaces with excellent visibility. Nonetheless, it is no easy challenge to watch one make a kill. These are shy birds that live in remote areas, and even should you be lucky enough to see the start of a hunt there is a strong chance that you will not witness the coup de grace, given the distance that the eagle may cover in the process. Furthermore, studies suggest that fewer than 20 per cent of the bird's hunting attempts end in success – a figure that varies with the prey, and with the age and experience of the eagle. The ancient art of falconry (see page 105) has revealed some of the techniques by which Golden Eagles capture their prey. However, this is in a controlled context and with a hand-reared bird, so may not tell the whole story. Video footage of wild birds has helped reveal more.

A Golden Eagle's hunting strategy varies with the terrain and the kind of prey it is targeting. Surprise is generally the key to success, with the approach determined by the way in which prey will try to escape: will it freeze, take flight or dash down a burrow? The acclaimed Golden Eagle biologist Jeff Watson (see page 124) identified seven key techniques. He named these as follows:

Above: A Golden Eagle flies low over a Scottish hillside, hoping to ambush a hare or game bird in the heather below.

Above: Once a Golden Eagle has spotted prey from a height, it begins to glide fast towards the target.

1. **High soar with glide attack**

The eagle soars high up, sometimes at 500m (1,640ft) or more, to spot its prey. Target located, it enters a long, low-angled glide – often for 1km (½ mile) or more – in which it gradually accelerates as it approaches its unsuspecting target. At the last moment it spreads its wings and tail to brake – often making a loud tearing sound in the process – and thrusts out its long legs to grab the quarry, either from the ground or, if the prey is a bird, just above the ground as it takes off. This technique also works when hunting from a high perch. It requires open country with long sightlines and works best for solitary or widely dispersed prey, such as hares or grouse.

2. **High soar with vertical stoop**

This is similar to the previous technique but used to capture flying birds, with the kill made in flight high above the ground. The eagle soars high, then stoops fast and almost vertically, like a Peregrine Falcon. Typical targets are large, relatively slow-flying birds, such as herons and geese. The victim is struck with the talons and knocked out of the air. If a flock of birds evades the first stoop they may fly higher to prevent the eagle from using its height advantage a second time.

3. Contour flight with short glide attack

This is probably the Golden Eagle's most common hunting technique and similar to that used by harriers. It is not so much about speed, as agility and reflex. The eagle quarters the ground in slow, low-level, flapping flight, often following the contours of a hillside and taking care not to make itself visible above the skyline. When it spots prey, it attacks with a short, low-angled glide – often repeating the manoeuvre if it misses the first time. The technique requires uneven topography with ridges or low vegetation, from behind which the eagle can spring its ambush. It serves for hunting communal prey, such as colonies of ground squirrels, with the individual target often selected only at the last second. A pair of eagles may work in tandem, each approaching the prey from a different direction, with the prey fleeing from one straight into the talons of the other.

4. Glide attack with tail-chase

This method starts with a long, low-angled stoop (as in 1 and 2, above), then continues when the quarry is flushed, with the eagle using its momentum and agility to match the twists and turns of its fleeing prey and, if the prey fails to find cover in time, to overhaul and seize it. It serves for hunting birds fleeing in the air and mammals along the ground. Again, a pair of eagles may work in tandem, one able to grab prey where the other misses: this approach is common with Golden Eagles hunting Mountain Hares in Scotland.

Below: A high-speed vertical stoop enables a Golden Eagle to ambush flying birds from above.

5. **Low flight with slow-descent attack**

Serving for slow-moving prey such as snakes, tortoises and Hedgehogs, this technique involves the bird quartering the ground slowly, then, when it spots its prey, stopping – often with a brief hover – and descending on its victim in a slow 'parachute' stoop. It demands little in the way of speed but may require more dexterity at the point of impact, especially in the case of snakes, where the head must be seized. Eagles may also use this technique when hunting a potentially dangerous mammal such as a Fox, remaining airborne just above it and only pressing home the attack if the target turns its head away. A fascinating video (see page 124) from Australia shows three Wedge-tailed Eagles (close relatives of the Golden Eagle) pursuing a full-grown Grey Kangaroo in this way – dropping down to strike with talons whenever it moves away, but rising back into the air whenever it turns to defend itself with powerful front claws. The kangaroo eventually escapes, but it is a close-run thing.

Below: A low, slow contour flight allows a Golden Eagle to drop suddenly on any prey that it flushes.

6. Low flight with sustained grip attack

This is the preferred technique for hunting ungulates such as deer. The eagle may make several passes over a group, which usually bunches in defence, before selecting its target and dropping down to seize it by the neck or back. It then clings on while the prey bolts, flapping its wings to slow down and unbalance its victim, while causing as much injury as possible with its talons. This brutal process may take several minutes, with the prey dropping to the ground through exhaustion, trauma and blood loss. The eagle may then try to transfer its killing grip to the skull to finish the job. Hunting this way is rare, and involves considerable risk to the eagle – both from the struggles of the much larger prey and, in some cases, from the aggression of its companions. It happens most often when other prey is unavailable, and when the terrain, such as steep crags, makes it hard for the quarry to escape.

Above: In the UK, the Golden Eagle is the only significant wild predator of the Red Fox.

7. Walk and grab attack

Eagles need not always be airborne to hunt. This technique involves simply walking up to the quarry and grabbing it, typically when it is hiding in undergrowth or even (in observations of mammals ranging from American Badgers to Pronghorn Antelope) beneath the legs of its mother. A pair of eagles may work in tandem: one bird pursuing the prey into a bush, for example, while its mate waits on the other side to grab it when it emerges.

Lamb slayers?
Predation by eagles on livestock

The issue of eagle predation on livestock – especially lambs – remains a vexed one. Many farmers regard the raptors as a lamb-killing menace. Conservationists, meanwhile, argue that this is a myth, perpetuated by lack of understanding and anecdote, and that it fuels a misguided persecution of the birds. Amid the controversy, the truth can be elusive.

Certainly, eagles do eat lambs. Remains found in their eyries offer irrefutable evidence of this. The great majority of such remains, however, have been scavenged. This is hardly surprising: some 30% of lambs in the highlands fall victim to bad weather or disease in their early days. The argument is thus over whether eagles ever *kill* lambs and, if so, how often. Newborn lambs, at around 5kg, fall well within the size range of eagles' prey, though push the very upper limit of what the birds can carry. In a few cases lambs are taken alive; bleeding or bruising around the talon marks on a carcass proves this. Even then, however, it is hard to prove that the victim was 'viable'. In other words, the lamb may already have been so weak that it was destined not to survive.

Studies of Scotland's eagles have concluded that they are responsible for up to 2.5% of lamb fatalities per year. Similar rates of lamb predation have been recorded among Golden Eagles in the USA, while in Sweden some 0.4% of Reindeer fawns – a key commercial livestock animal in Scandinavia – are, on average, lost to eagles. Figures vary from year to year. Nowhere, however, does evidence suggest that eagles killing lambs represents habitual predation. More likely, it is occasional opportunism. Furthermore, the losses are trivial in commercial terms: a 2010 Scottish Natural Heritage study concluded that eagle predation had 'minimum impact' on livestock farming.

Nonetheless, the hostility persists. In a 2014 North Argyll survey, around 80% of sheep farmers questioned believed their business had suffered as a result of White-tailed Eagle predation. There are still calls for eagles to be 'controlled' and fierce protests have greeted attempts to reintroduce them in Scotland and Ireland. Where eagles have brought proven economic benefits, such as on Mull where White-tailed Eagles attract millions in tourist spending each year, attitudes are changing. Elsewhere, conservationists still have a battle on their hands.

Above: A White-tailed Eagle scavenges from the carcass of a sheep that died of natural causes.

The White-tailed Eagle menu

The White-tailed Eagle is a larger bird than the Golden Eagle and requires on average more food – some 500–600g (18–21oz) a day. However, due to its longer gut and more efficient digestive system it can survive longer without feeding. It also has a large, flexible crop, which allows it to store food for later consumption. Both these adaptations enable it to live at higher densities than Golden Eagles, with less intense competition between individual birds.

Like the Golden Eagle, the White-tailed Eagle takes a variety of prey species across its range – although its preferred prey seldom coincides with that of its smaller, more aggressive cousin, so the two seldom compete over food. Its diet in a given location tends to be broader than that of the Golden Eagle, and combines fish, sea birds and other live prey with plentiful scavenging. Studies on the Scottish island of Mull, for example, reveal that more than 40 species of bird, mammal and fish are on the local menu during the breeding season.

Above: The White-tailed Eagle captures a wide variety of fish, plucking them with its talons from close to the surface.

The main food items for a White-tailed Eagle can be grouped as follows:

Fish A variety of fish, both marine ones such as pollock and lumpsucker and freshwater ones such as pike, perch and salmon. Catches range from 0.5 to 3kg (1–6½lb) in weight, although this powerful raptor may capture a fish of more than 3kg (6½lb) and tow it to the shore if it is too heavy to lift. It will readily raid commercial fish farms – notably carp ponds in eastern Europe. In Kamchatka it congregates alongside the even larger Steller's Sea Eagle at salmon-spawning rivers in September and October, both species feeding side by side on the abundant dead and dying fish. On Hokkaido Island, Japan, the two species also gather to fish the Pacific Cod (*Gadus macrocephalus*) that mass in the Rausu Sea and the Nemuro Straits in February and support a local fishery, where the eagles often receive handouts. Alaska Pollock (*Theragra chalcogramma*) is another important winter food source in this part of the world.

Below: In Scotland Fulmars are an important prey species for White-tailed Eagles, which pluck the seabirds from their cliff-top nests.

Birds The dominant food in many regions. One study in Norway put birds at 64 per cent of the total and fish at 33.3 per cent. The main targets are waterfowl such as ducks, coots and grebes, and sea birds such as gulls, auks and Fulmars. Local preference depends upon season and what is most easily available. On Scotland's Isle of Mull, Fulmars, Shags and Eider Ducks regularly fall prey; for wintering eagles on the Danube Delta, coots are a favourite; and on one island in Estonia, the target is mainly Cormorants. The eagles will plunder breeding colonies to take eggs, nestlings and sometimes adults. Not all victims are water birds: other species recorded on the Mull menu range from Red Grouse to Mistle Thrush and even Cuckoo.

Mammals and other prey Most mammals eaten by White-tailed Eagles are already dead before the bird gets stuck in. However, this species is well capable of capturing furry prey and has been recorded killing everything from Water Voles to young Reindeer. It is not as adept as the Golden Eagle in this kind of hunting, so mammals form a smaller proportion of its diet, but is nonetheless a canny opportunist that will happily kill any mammal it can eat. Mammals recorded on the Isle of Mull includes rats, Rabbit, Roe Deer and even American Mink. Other live prey recorded ranges from snakes and frogs to cuttlefish and even freshwater mussels. Unfortunately, this bird's capacity for killing larger mammals has brought problems with farmers, many of whom still see it as a significant predator of sheep and lambs. All evidence suggests that this happens only very rarely, however, and that the vast majority of livestock consumed by White-tailed Eagles comes in the form of carrion (see page 60).

Above: White-tailed Eagles obtain much of their food by scavenging from carcasses.

Carrion White-tailed Eagles take a much larger proportion of carrion in their diet than do Golden Eagles, especially during the winter months when in many regions it becomes their staple. The carrion ranges from dead fish on the shoreline, to livestock, deer and other larger animals found inland. Other mammals scavenged, when found, include seals, cetaceans and – brace yourself – even human beings. In parts of the world with higher White-tailed Eagle populations, large numbers (50 or more) may gather at a carrion bonanza, such as a beached whale or a mass gathering of dead salmon at a spawning river.

Below: A large carcass, such as this Roe Deer, may attract several White-tailed Eagles, along with smaller scavengers such as the Magpie and Raven seen here.

White-tailed Eagle diet: an RSPB study

The RSPB monitors the breeding season diet of White-tailed Eagles in Scotland by collecting prey remains from the nest after the young have fledged. In 2005 more than 800 items were collected from 22 successful nest-sites. More than 40 different birds, mammal and fish were identified – as shown in the table below. Sea birds dominated, with Fulmars contributing almost 50% of all items recorded.

Birds		
Diver species	Red-breasted Merganser	Razorbill
Fulmar	Red Grouse	Black Guillemot
Manx Shearwater	Pheasant	Puffin
Gannet	Oystercatcher	Cuckoo
Cormorant	Curlew	Mistle Thrush
Shag	Snipe	Raven
Grey Heron	Common Gull	Hooded Crow
Greylag Goose	Herring Gull	
Mallard	Lesser Black-backed Gull	
Eider	Great Black-backed Gull	
Shelduck	Guillemot	

Mammals		
Brown Rat	Rabbit	Roe Deer calf
Mountain Hare	Mink	Red Deer calf
Irish Hare	Lamb	

Fish		
Lumpsucker	Ling	Conger Eel
Mackerel	Cod	
Dogfish sp.	Hake	

How White-tailed Eagles hunt

These huge birds catch much of their prey in the water. They usually spot their target from a raised perch, such as an overhanging tree or clifftop, or while circling overhead. They then glide down to pluck it from the surface, extending their long legs, talons together, just before the moment of impact. Often an eagle will hover briefly just above the surface to position itself before the final strike. Unlike the Osprey, an even more specialised

fish catcher, it seldom plunges below the water or immerses itself.

This one-strike technique works for fish, and also for non-diving water birds such as Mallard. Diving birds, however, such as auks, coots and diving ducks, slip below the surface if they spot the eagle coming. An eagle often makes repeated dives for such birds, swooping down on the target every time it comes back up. Eventually, exhausted, the bird is forced back to the surface where it becomes – often literally – a sitting duck. When hunting Fulmars and other birds that breed on cliffs, a White-tailed Eagle may glide along the top of the cliff, out of sight of the birds nesting on the cliff face, then suddenly flip over the edge and hope to grab one.

Above: A White-tailed Eagle plucks prey from the water's surface by lunging forward with outstretched legs.

A free meal

Like other sea eagle species, the White-tailed Eagle is also an accomplished kleptoparasite. In lay terms this means that it will rob other animals of their hard-earned catch. Victims of this piracy include other fish-catching

Above: A Steller's Sea Eagle and two White-tailed Eagles battle for possession of a fish in Hokkaido, Japan.

birds, such as Ospreys, herons and cormorants, and even fish-eating mammals such as otters. An eagle will watch the fisher from a concealed position, then, once the catch is made, swoop down to harass and intimidate it – either in the air or on the ground – until it relinquishes its catch. Where White-tailed Eagles gather at an abundant food source, such as a large carcass, they will also steal food from one another, often entering into violent flapping squabbles in which age and experience help to establish a pecking order – literally.

Where White-tailed Eagles are not persecuted, they can live alongside humans and become bold enough to scavenge for handouts. They often hang around abattoirs and fishing plants, feeding on any discarded waste. In some places, including Japan and eastern Europe, they may perch near fishermen and wait for any discarded catch to be flung their way. Evidence suggests that they will do this only with familiar individuals, however, and that they keep their distance if strangers are present. This learning capacity has seen them respond to the sound of a wildfowler's gun in Belarus, and recognise individual fishing boats in both Norway and Scotland whose skippers are prepared to fling them the odd free meal. Such events can also make for an exciting tourist experience (see page 121). Either way, they certainly give the White-tailed Eagle an edge over the Golden Eagle, which is far too wary of humans to exploit such opportunities.

Eagle versus eagle

Golden Eagles and White-tailed Eagles often live side by side. This has raised questions about how well the two species can coexist – questions that become serious considerations when, as in Scotland, the White-tailed Eagle is reintroduced to areas where the Golden Eagle was already established (see page 117).

Thankfully, it seems that the two birds differ sufficiently in their feeding behaviour so as not to compete seriously. Each can generally get along doing its own thing without worrying about the other. However, no predator likes another predator, and there is no love lost between these two birds. If they run into one another it may end in blows – and occasionally fatal ones. White-tailed Eagles have been found killed by a Golden Eagle's talons and Golden Eagles have been found drowned by White-tailed Eagles.

Generally, the only circumstances in which the two huge raptors are forced into close proximity is when scavenging from the same carcass. This happens most often in winter. On such occasions a Golden Eagle tends to be dominant: although slightly smaller than a White-tailed Eagle, it is more aggressive and has more fearsome talons. Such meetings are rare in Scotland but in some parts of the world happen more regularly – notably in eastern Asia and Japan, where a third player, the huge Steller's Sea Eagle, may join the drama. This massive bird, with its intimidating bill, tends to dominate both the others, although Golden Eagles never back down easily.

Neither species is fond of other predatory birds, which will harass eagles and try to drive them away. A sighting of either eagle in Scotland often includes other birds, such as Ravens, Buzzards or Peregrine Falcons, which are mobbing the huge raptors. Eagles will attack and kill any other birds, if they can. These smaller species know that – but in open flight, with their smaller size and greater agility, they have the upper hand. Eagles also sometimes meet predatory mammals at a carcass, and have been observed feeding alongside Red Foxes.

Below: A Golden Eagle and a White-tailed Eagle squabble over a carcass.

The Next Generation

The defining challenge for any eagle is to usher the next generation into the world. Our two UK species are typical of all eagles worldwide when it comes to breeding. They form strong, often lifelong pair bonds, in which both partners work closely to produce one brood a year. It is hard work: the job starts in spring with the building or refurbishment of the huge nest, and continues through a six-month process of laying and incubating eggs, hatching and raising chicks, and finally helping the fledged youngsters take their first faltering steps – or rather flaps – into the world beyond. Six months later it starts all over again. Success is never certain: only about half the eggs laid by both species result in fully fledged young eagles.

Getting together

The two UK eagle species reach breeding maturity at around five years, at which point they look for a mate. Like most eagles, both are monogamous. A pair often mates for life, staying together until one partner dies. A bird that loses its mate, however, usually finds a replacement fairly quickly.

In spring, adults perform aerial courtship displays in order to attract a mate or reaffirm the pair bond with their existing mate. In a male Golden Eagle's spectacular 'sky dance', which also serves as a territorial display, he makes a series of steep dives – up to 20 in succession – in an undulating pattern across the sky. To attract a new female, he will also carry up a rock in his talons, drop it from a height, then swoop down to recapture it in mid-air, repeating this manoeuvre up to three times. His mate may join him, performing a similar aerobatic routine with clods of earth.

Established pairs do not usually go to such dramatic lengths, but upon returning to their breeding territory after winter wanderings they renew their bond with

Above: A pair of White-tailed Eagles lock talons in their courtship flight.

Opposite: A White-tailed Eagle delivers food directly into the begging bill of one of its nestlings.

'mutual soaring', in which both birds take to the air simultaneously to circle high over their nesting territory. They may also dive and chase after one another in mock attacks, often sweeping past within a few metres of each other and even rolling to present their talons.

The mutual aerial displays of White-tailed Eagles are even more impressive. Amid the diving and rolling, the two birds may lock talons in mid-air and cartwheel towards the ground, only pulling out of the dive with a few metres to go. Indeed, White-tailed Eagles are generally more demonstrative and much more vocal birds than Golden Eagles. The male calls frequently, especially early in the morning, with a high-pitched, dog-like yapping, and the pair – as is common in other *Haliaeetus* sea eagles – may call together in duet, flinging back their heads as they do so. When not soaring they loaf around together, sitting for long periods in close proximity.

Mating generally takes place as the birds begin the process of nest building – typically about six weeks before the eggs are laid, although the pair may continue to copulate even during the incubation period. In Golden Eagles, copulation often follows a passage of mutual high soaring, the female descending to land on a rock or high ground – although not at the eyrie – and the male arriving shortly afterwards to mount her. The act takes some 10–20 seconds, after which the birds may sit together for a while.

Above: A pair of White-tailed Eagles renews their bonds with 'mutual soaring'.

Home on the range

Above: The home range of a Golden Eagle comprises vast tracts of open country.

Golden Eagles and White-tailed Eagles, like all eagles, need plenty of space. A breeding pair generally occupies the same area all its life. This area is known as the home range, and must meet all their hunting and breeding needs. A home range is often defined by topographical features, such as ridges and valleys, and varies in size according to the terrain. In Golden Eagles it may be as small as 20km² (8 square miles) in areas of good habitat and high prey density, such as the Isle of Mull, or as much as 200km² (80 square miles) in less productive areas. The average in Scotland is around 50km² (19 square miles), with roughly 10–60 pairs of Golden Eagle per 1,000km² (386 square miles). White-tailed Eagles have a similar-sized home range, with similar variations according to the quality of habitat.

Within its home range each pair of eagles maintains a smaller breeding territory, where it sites its nests. It is actively territorial in defence of this area, performing aerial displays to deter rival pairs and showing downright aggression towards wandering immature birds. These birds, known as 'floaters', have much larger ranges. Studies in Switzerland found that wandering immature Golden Eagles may cover an accumulated range up to 15,000km² (5792 square miles) during their first two years, with this figure falling to 2,000–4,000km² (772-1544 square miles) during years three and four. During this time they use several base areas, often moving from one to another as resident pairs drive them away. Males tend to wander further than females.

In the UK, both the Golden Eagle and White-tailed Eagle are sedentary (ie non-migratory) species. After reaching breeding maturity they seldom leave their home range. In other parts of the world, however, where the home range does not offer enough food during winter, they become migrants. In North America, Golden Eagles from Alaska and northern Canada migrate thousands of kilometres south to the south-western USA, for example, while White-tailed Eagles from north-eastern Europe make similar journeys to central-southern Europe. These migrant birds establish new home ranges in their winter-quarters and then return again in spring to their breeding home ranges. During migration, they may be more tolerant of each other's company. One study of migrating Golden Eagles roosting on pylons in Idaho, USA, found 56 of 85 pylons on one stretch occupied. Clearly personal space for these birds was not an issue.

Nesting

Eagles need a lot of space in which to nest. In Scotland the density of nesting Golden Eagles averages out at 20 pairs per 1,000km² (386 square miles). The extent to which one pair will tolerate its neighbours varies with the terrain and the abundance of prey: studies in Norway have found a minimum distance of 16km (10 miles) between two nesting pairs of Golden Eagles; in the Swiss Alps, where prey is more plentiful, this distance is just 8km (5 miles). White-tailed Eagles require slightly less space, with a pair's average breeding territory measuring some 30–70km² (12–17 square miles).

The siting of a nest is critical to a pair's breeding success. In Scotland and across much of northern mainland Europe, Golden Eagles tend to choose remote areas inland, while White-tailed Eagles choose sites along the coast. However, each bird has specific requirements. Scottish Golden Eagles invariably nest on cliffs, typically on an inaccessible ledge, too high above the ground and too far from the top to allow any large mammal – including humans – to get at the eggs or nestlings. They avoid mountaintops, however, as they like the option of hunting at a higher altitude than their nest, which enables them more easily to transport heavy prey

Below: A Golden Eagle takes flight from its eyrie, high on an inaccessible cliff face.

by gliding with it downhill. In more northerly parts of their range, such as Alaska, the nest-site is generally south-facing, so that the chicks can enjoy the sun's direct heat through the day. In more southern regions, such as Oman, it is generally north-facing, so that they are not too exposed to the fierce heat of the day.

Golden Eagles do not nest only on cliffs. They may also nest on the ground, usually on remote, boulder-strewn slopes with fine all-round visibility. In some parts of their range – the forested peatlands of Belarus and the Baltic States, for example, and some wooded parts of North America, including Wyoming and Washington – they nest in trees, usually placing their eyrie some 12m (40ft) above the ground in a large tree such as a Douglas Fir. Golden Eagles in America have even been known to nest on electricity pylons.

White-tailed Eagles are more habitual tree nesters, although they will also nest on sea cliffs and, occasionally, on the ground. They tend to choose tall trees in an undisturbed forest not far from water, either on a coast or beside a lake.

In both species the nest itself is a massive structure, with tree nests being larger and deeper than cliff nests. Golden Eagle nests average 2m (6½ft) deep by 1.5m (5ft) across, and weigh up to 250kg (550lb). White-tailed Eagle nests

Above: White-tailed Eagles generally build their eyrie in a large tree.

Above: A pair of Bald Eagles tend their chick at the nest. This American species, closely related to the White-tailed Eagle, builds the largest known stick nests of any bird.

are no smaller, and may grow so large that branches break beneath them. The largest stick nest built by any bird is that of the Bald Eagle – a very close relative of the White-tailed Eagle – with the world record belonging to a nest in St Petersburg, Florida, USA, which measured an impressive 2.9m (9½ft) wide by 6m (20ft) deep, and weighed an estimated 2 tonnes.

The essential building materials for these great edifices are sticks. White-tailed Eagles also take driftwood and use, on average, slightly larger sticks than Golden Eagles, measuring up to 1.5m (5ft) long by 5cm (2in) across. One White-tailed Eagle nest that fell from a tree on the Isle of Mull contained 2,900 branches and weighed 240kg (530lb). A pair upholsters their nest with small grasses, rushes, heather and – in the case of the White-tailed Eagle – seaweed. Both birds share the work, with the male generally doing more fetching and carrying, and the female more arranging. As the time of laying approaches, sprigs of fresh greenery are added. This final embellishment is continually replenished during incubation and the earliest days of the chicks. It is thought to advertise occupancy of the eyrie and also to promote nest hygiene. Indeed, the birds may deliberately select aromatic plants, whose fragrance helps deter parasites.

One reason why some eagle nests grow so large is that they are generally used repeatedly, with the pair adding more material each year. One White-tailed Eagle nest in Iceland, constructed on the ground, was continuously occupied for more than 150 years. However, eagles do not always use the same nest. A pair may maintain several nests within its territory, with up to ten being recorded for Golden Eagles in Scotland. The birds may switch between these nests from one year to the next, or may stay for several years with just one favourite. Each season the birds may refurbish up to three nests in preparation for laying, then choose the most suitable..

Eggs and incubation

Eagles lay their eggs in early spring. In Scotland this can mean any time from early March to mid-April for both species. Worldwide, the average date depends upon latitude, with more northerly birds generally laying later in the year than southerly ones. The earliest known average laying date for Golden Eagles is 3 December, in Oman; the latest is 7 May, in Alaska.

Both species lay anything from one to four eggs, with the average being two. The eggs are a little rounder than those of a hen and more than twice as big, measuring on average 7.5cm (3in) long and 5.9cm (2½in) across, for both species. The White-tailed Eagle's eggs, at around 123g (4½oz), are a little lighter than the Golden Eagle's, which average 145g (5oz). (A medium-sized hen's egg weighs 50g/1¾oz.) The Golden Eagle's eggs are white and usually blotched with reddish-brown spots. The White-tailed Eagle's are also white, but plainer and sometimes with a yellowish tinge.

Below: This Golden Eagle clutch in the Scottish Highlands shows how the eggs may vary in colour.

Above: An adult Golden Eagle incubating its eggs in a pine tree eyrie.

In both species the female lays her eggs at intervals of 3–5 days, which means their hatching is similarly staggered. Golden Eagles incubate their eggs for 41–45 days and White-tailed Eagles for a little less, at 38 days. The female in both species does most of this work, with the male relieving her for short periods – up to 27 per cent of the time in Scottish White-tailed Eagles – although never at night. Unlike in some other birds, the female does not rely upon food from the male, but takes breaks from incubating in order to hunt for herself. If the male does bring anything back, he will generally leave it on a rock or other vantage point nearby rather than taking it direct to the eyrie.

Eagle voices

For such large, powerful birds, most eagles have surprisingly unimpressive voices. Sea eagles of the *Haliaeetus* genus are louder than most, however, and certainly the White-tailed Eagle is much the more vocal of the two UK eagles. Its high-pitched call, consisting of a sequence of shrill yelping notes, is most often heard during the breeding season, when a pair may call together in duet, sometimes pointing their bills skywards as the call rises in frequency and pitch. Golden Eagles have a more feeble voice and use it much less often. Adults tend only to make their weak, high-pitched whistle – sometimes described as 'puppy-like' – when agitated or, occasionally, when greeting a mate. Hungry youngsters are louder, and their loud 'yip-yip' food-begging call at the nest can carry for some distance.

Above: A White-tailed Eagle throws back its head when uttering its piercing territorial call.

Hatching and growing

Hatching is a slow, arduous process. In Golden Eagles it takes around 37 hours, with a hatchling's first noises audible from inside the egg some 15 hours before it starts breaking out of the shell. A newly hatched chick weighs around 110g (4oz) – about the weight of a small dove – and is covered in fluffy white down. For the first ten days chicks lie at the bottom of the nest, where they are kept warm by the continually brooding parents. The female does the bulk of brooding during this period, seldom leaving the nest for the first 45 days after the young have hatched. The male perches away from the nest and goes off hunting for his new charges, providing some 90 per cent of the food during these early days. After 50 days, once the eaglets have the nest to themselves, the two parents share the hunting duties.

Well provisioned from day one, the eaglets pile on the weight, reaching 500g (18oz) by ten days. By 20 days they are standing up. They also become steadily noisier,

Below: A Golden Eagle feeds its young nestling.

Above: Two-week-old Golden Eagle nestlings in their Scottish eyrie, early May.

Below: A young White-tailed Eagle in the process of shedding its down feathers.

progressing from a soft *chirp* after first hatching to louder, harsher calls from about 20 days. Growth continues apace. The adults feed the chicks directly, with the female (usually) tearing off flesh from whatever prey has been brought to the nest and stuffing it directly into the eaglets' gaping bills. Female nestlings consume more than males. By 20 days the youngsters have started 'mantling' – spreading their wings and tail protectively over their food to keep it to themselves – and by 20 days they have learned to defecate over the edge of the nest. After around 30 days they are tearing at their own food. By 40 days the female stops perching on the nest and the parents simply dump the prey there for the chicks to help themselves. By this time the rapid growth increase of the youngsters has levelled off.

As the chicks gain size they start to look more like eagles. By around 25 days dark contour feathers start growing among the white down feathers, giving a bird a patchy, piebald appearance. From 50 days dark brown feathers sprout from the same sockets as the down feathers, with long wing and tail feathers giving the bird a more adult appearance. The feet, meanwhile, change from flesh coloured at hatching, to first grey, then black and ultimately yellow. If surprised at the nest, the youngsters will fall back and strike upwards with their feet, hissing aggressively.

Cain and Abel

We may admire eagles as 'noble' birds, but there is one aspect of their biology on which many prefer not to dwell. This avian elephant in the room is siblicide: the killing of one hatchling by another. Known as 'cainism', from its biblical model, the practice is common to most *Aquila* species and the Golden Eagle is no exception. It comes down to size and timing. Due to the staggered hatching of a brood, the first hatchling generally has a 50 per cent size advantage by the time the second arrives 3–4 days later. This firstborn uses its physical superiority to bully its smaller sibling out of food brought by the parents. Between meals it extends this aggression into physical attacks, repeatedly pecking the smaller one and soon causing serious wounds. The weaker sibling soon stops begging for food and either succumbs to death through starvation or dies of its injuries; the older chick may even force its miserable sibling right out of the nest. Throughout this brutal process, the parents do not intervene.

Above: A Golden Eagle chick attacks its younger sibling on the nest, Carpathian Mountains, Poland.

Even putting aside the unpleasantness (to us) of an animal turning on its own kith and kin, you might reasonably wonder what biological purpose such an apparently wasteful practice could possibly serve. To understand this, we must put aside sentiment and accept that nothing in nature evolves unless it works. The explanation accepted by most scientists is that the second hatchling (and the third, if the brood is that large) functions mostly as a back-up. To achieve breeding success, a pair of eagles needs to raise only one chick to maturity. However, with food unreliable and young hatchlings vulnerable during their early days, it makes sense to have another chick waiting in the wings. Once the first chick hatches successfully and starts growing healthily, a second is no longer required; its death is simply collateral damage. Indeed, it may save the parents some hard work further down the line.

In some *Aquila* species, including Verreaux's and Tawny Eagles, cainism is 'obligate' – that is, their breeding biology depends upon it. In Golden Eagles, however, it is 'facultative', which means that it occurs as circumstances dictate. Behaviour varies from one part of the world to another: Golden Eagles in parts of North America regularly raise two or more chicks; in Scotland, however, siblicide is the norm, with the survival of a second hatchling occurring in no more than 20 per cent of nests and, in some areas, in as few as 4 per cent. The die is generally cast during the first 20 days. If the second chick survives this far, it may become strong enough to hold its own and continue all the way to fledging. In Scottish Golden Eagles, the prevalance of siblicide correlates with food supply. In good times, when the parents can provide enough food for two chicks, both may reach maturity. This result is a happy bonus.

Siblicide is not common to all eagles and indeed is rare among *Haliaeetus* sea eagles. Thus White-Tailed Eagles enjoy a far less brutal life as hatchlings than their Golden Eagle neighbours: in normal conditions most pairs rear two or more chicks to maturity, although the first hatched is invariably the dominant one and may show some aggression towards its smaller sibling. Siblicide also occurs in other predatory birds, including gulls, skuas and owls.

Off and away

Above: A four-week old Golden Eagle chick starts to stretch its growing wings; beside it in the nest is an unhatched egg.

Below: A Golden Eagle with its half-grown chick; flight feathers are beginning to grow.

By 20 days the eaglets are making the first feeble flaps of their stumpy little wings. As these wings grow and develop in structure, sprouting flight feathers, the exercises become more regular. By 40 days the eaglets are flapping vigorously and spending more time at the edge of the nest, contemplating the huge world that beckons from beyond. Fledging – the permanent departure from the nest – comes in Golden Eagles at 8–9 weeks, and in White-tailed Eagles at 10–11 weeks. The precise timing varies from one part of the world to another: studies suggest that it occurs at 66–75 days for Golden Eagles in Idaho, USA, for instance, but at 70–81 days in Scotland.

By now, the parents are placing food a short distance away from the nest to encourage the youngsters to leave. Finally a hatchling will pluck up courage and take the plunge. It may jump off of its own volition and glide

downwards a short distance, or it may be blown off the edge of the nest as it raises its wings. Either way, the unsteady first flight generally ends with an awkward crash landing. For the next few weeks the fledglings generally remain within 100m (328ft) of the nest, taking up a favourite perch where the parents continue to bring them food. They sit still for long periods as their flight feathers continue to grow, making occasional practice flights. Some 18–20 days after fledging they will feel confident enough to make their first circling flight, although it is a couple of months before they can gain height as efficiently as their parents.

By about 60 days after fledging an eaglet is making its first hunting forays. It will accompany its parents at first, and it is not uncommon to see three birds airborne at this time, with the fledgling now distinguishable from its parents only by plumage. As its success in finding food increases, the youngster begins to shun the attention of its parents. Within about four months – which, in Scotland, means mid to late autumn – it is effectively independent.

Wandering

The next step for a newly independent young eagle is to move away from the familiar landscape of its parents' territory. This first winter in the life of a young eagle brings perhaps its greatest challenge: surviving alone in strange new lands, with no experience and resources thin on the ground. Hunting skills take much longer to master than flight skills, and for this first winter eaglets of both species are heavily dependent on finding carrion. At first the immature eagles will move just a short distance – studies of Golden Eagles in Israel have shown that they typically settle around 12km (7½ miles) from the nest in which they were raised. Soon, however,

Below: A young White-tailed Eagle, having recently left its parents, contemplates its first winter alone.

Costume change

Above: This immature White-tailed Eagle has not yet acquired the pale head, white tail and completely yellow bill of adulthood.

Like all birds, eagles renew their plumage throughout their life via the process of moult. For their first five or so years, until they reach breeding maturity, the colour and pattern of this plumage changes with each moult. Immature birds are thus easily distinguished from adults – although it can be hard to know exactly how old the youngsters are, as their plumage varies as much by individual as by age.

Juvenile Golden Eagles differ from their parents by having white patches on their wings, at the base of the primaries and secondaries, and a white patch on the tail, which extends from the base to the dark terminal band. They retain this plumage for their first winter, then undergo two full moults as they mature, The extent of the white generally decreases until, by their sixth or seventh summer, they have acquired their complete all-brown adult plumage.

White-tailed Eagles, by contrast, are darker when younger. As they mature, they gain rather than lose white feathers in the tail, retaining a dark

they wander further afield, with females travelling a greater distance than males. In some populations these movements take the form of lengthy migrations: studies of Golden Eagles in Denali National Park in Alaska showed that youngsters moved an average of more than 5,500km (3,418 miles) during their first year.

Much about these early years in an eagle's life remains a mystery. If the young eagle survives its first winter, then for the next 2–3 years it will continue to travel widely. After this initial exploratory and nomadic phase, it usually returns to the area in which it was raised and, once it has reached breeding maturity, settles down in a new territory of its own. Breeding generally starts at five years, occasionally earlier. One radio-tagged juvenile Golden Eagle in Spain travelled around a range of 16,000km^2 (6,178 square miles) in its first three years of independence, but ultimately settled in a vacant territory just 26km (16 miles) from where it was raised.

terminal band until their fifth or sixth summer when the tail becomes pure white. They have a darker head, which becomes paler with each moult, and their bill is dark grey, not acquiring its bright yellow until breeding maturity. As with Golden Eagles, these plumage differences between adult and youngster are thought to allay any aggression directed by the former at the latter.

Once in adult attire, eagles continue to moult throughout their life in order to replace lost, worn and damaged feathers. Most feathers are moulted between April and September, with a peak in July/August. A complete feather change takes two moulting seasons. Moult of the smaller contour feathers begins around the head and proceeds from front to back. With the larger wing and tail feathers, it begins with the innermost and proceeds outwards. The process slows down during winter, when birds need to retain maximum energy and flight efficiency to survive this most challenging season.

Above: An immature Golden Eagle shows bold white markings on its wings and tail. The extent of the white shrinks with each moult.

A long life

Growing up is a tough test for any eagle. Fewer than half of Golden Eagle hatchlings are thought to overcome the challenges of hatching, fledging and dispersal to reach maturity. If an eaglet can negotiate those early years without mishap, however, it may go on to reach a ripe old age. The lifespan of Golden Eagles in the wild varies from one population to another, averaging some 15–25 years, with the record belonging to a 32-year-old bird that was ringed as a nestling in Sweden. For White-tailed Eagles the average lifespan in the UK is 21 years, with the oldest recorded individual also being 32. Both birds may live significantly longer in captivity, however, with one captive Golden Eagle in America reaching the impressive age of 46.

Threats and Enemies

You might think that eagles would have little to fear – and it is true that the largest species, including both the Golden Eagle and the White-tailed Eagle, have few serious natural enemies. Nonetheless, surviving by your wits in some of the world's wildest places is never easy for any predator: there is the weather to contend with, for a start, while prey seldom gives in without a fight. Sadly, humans have made the challenge much harder. Whether through deliberately persecuting the birds as our competitors, or by ruining their landscape and littering it with hazards and obstacles, it is we who pose by far the gravest dangers to eagles. Indeed, we hold their fate in our hands.

Natural dangers

Most eagles die far from human eyes, with the causes of their deaths unreported. We can be reasonably sure, however, that both adult Golden and White-tailed Eagles are such daunting adversaries that very few other animals will attack them. The rare records of either species killed in such attacks generally reflect exceptional circumstances.

Above: Two White-tailed Eagles squabble over a carcass, Poland.

Other eagles

The wild animal most likely to kill an eagle is another eagle. Both Golden and White-tailed Eagles sometimes perish during territorial battles with others of their own kind. These clashes most often occur when young birds return to their natal area to claim a new breeding territory and attempt to oust resident birds. While disputes are often settled by display, sometimes the birds may come to blows, with their talons capable of inflicting lethal wounds. The two species may also clash with each other (see page 67), sometimes with fatal consequences. In areas where Golden Eagles share territory with other large *Aquila* species, such as Bonelli's Eagles or Steppe Eagles, they generally dominate by virtue of their superior size and power.

Opposite: A young White-tailed Eagle on the Norwegian coast nurses a broken wing. Eagles can sustain serious injuries in collisions.

Other wild animals

Both eagle species do occasionally fall victim to some of the larger predatory mammals with which they coexist, including Wolverines, Snow Leopards, Cougars and Brown Bears. With an element of surprise, such powerful animals can easily overcome an eagle, but the circumstances in which such an encounter might arise must be very rare. Generally it is pure opportunism, resulting from the predator ambushing an eagle feeding on the ground. Birds killed in this way are most likely to be inexperienced subadults. A trawl of YouTube reveals some extraordinary encounters captured on amateur

Above: Ravens surround a White-tailed Eagle feeding on the ground. In such circumstances the eagle may be vulnerable to attack by other large predators.

video. In one, a Leopard in Botswana captures an unwary African Hawk Eagle feeding on the ground; in another, a Golden Eagle makes a narrow escape from a Bobcat that steals its kill.

Eagles may also come a cropper when prey fights back. Golden Eagles on the Isle of Rum have been kicked to death by Red Deer hinds defending their calves. Among more unusual records from North America are one of a Golden Eagle fatally pierced by the quills of a porcupine it was attacking, and another stabbed to death by a Great Blue Heron it was trying to capture. Both White-tailed and

Golden Eagles may also come off worse while hunting Fulmars: these cliff-nesting seabirds vomit up a foul-smelling stomach oil in self-defence, which may leave a raptor's feathers so clogged that it is incapable of flying and so drowns.

An unattended eagle nest may also fall prey to a daring opportunist. The likes of Hooded Crows or even Pine Martens might steal an egg, while youngsters are vulnerable to predatory birds such as Buzzards, Ravens and large owls. Any predator raiding an eagle nest does so at its own peril. Amateur video footage from Canada shows Bald Eagles driving away a Black Bear that attempts to climb their nest tree, striking it with their talons. Opportunities arise most often when the adults have been scared away; evidence suggests that nest predation is most common in areas of increased human disturbance.

Above: A Red Deer hind will protect its calf aggressively from an attack by an eagle or any other predator.

Other natural dangers

Many eagles live in remote regions where the weather can be rough. Persistent rain and unseasonal cold (ever had a summer holiday in the Scottish Highlands?) can endanger eggs and nestlings, which require constant incubation from their parents. Rain and cloud can deprive eagles of the thermals they need for soaring, restricting their hunting options. Rain, mist and falling snow also make prey harder to spot – and also often ensure that it lies low.

Below: Persistent rain causes difficulties for eagles, not allowing them the thermals they need on which to soar in search of prey.

An eagle that cannot hunt goes hungry – or at least its chicks do. Starvation is a common fate for inexperienced youngsters trying to find food during their first winter. One study in Denali National Park, Alaska, found that 11 of 16 young Golden Eagles monitored perished in this way. Among weakened birds disease can also take its toll. Avian cholera – caused by the *Pasteurella meltocida* bacterium – may affect any raptors that eat waterfowl, including both White-tailed and Golden Eagles.

Perils from people

It is a sad reality that the natural dangers eagles face amount to little compared with those introduced to their environment by people. Dealing with predators, weather and disease is part of an eagle's evolutionary make-up. Dealing with traps, bullets, pesticides, poisons and power lines is not; nor is living in a landscape in which the native plants have been removed and prey species eradicated. To grasp how such anthropogenic threats outweigh the natural ones, you need only look at a ten-year survey of Golden Eagle mortality in Spain: of the 266 deaths recorded from 1980 to 1990, only six were not attributed, in some way, to people.

Endangered spaces

Eagles, as we have seen, need plenty of space. What is more, they need the right kind of space – that is, the habitats in which they evolved must be broadly intact, providing suitable terrain in which to find food and rear chicks. The destruction or modification of these habitats has been a critical factor in the decline of many eagle species around the globe.

Below: A Golden Eagle looks out over a Highlands habitat that has been transformed by forestry plantations.

The Golden Eagle is particularly vulnerable to habitat loss. Development, fuelled by the demands of a burgeoning human population, has helped speed the bird's retreat from much of its former range, including in Britain, mainland Europe and the eastern United States. It is not simply about losing green space – after all, many places in which Golden Eagles live are too rugged for cities, roads or industry. More often, it is about the replacement of one kind of green space by another, less welcome, kind.

Afforestation is a particular problem. Commercial plantations of non-native trees such as Sitka Spruce create a dense, closed-canopy habitat in which the eagles cannot hunt and which, in any case, no longer supports the hares and other prey animals that they would be after if they could. This process has transformed much of Scotland since 1954, and has also affected eagle habitat in France, Portugal and Japan. White-tailed Eagles, meanwhile, have suffered from deforestation in parts of their range, with the loss of suitable nesting trees along, for example, the Danube floodplain in Hungary.

Above: Intensive grazing by sheep depletes upland regions of natural ground cover, reducing their capacity to support the eagles' key prey species.

Livestock farming can also damage eagle habitat. Some Scottish uplands heavily grazed by sheep have lost their heather cover to grass, which does not support key eagle prey species. Indeed, on some grouse moors, Mountain Hares – the eagles' staple diet – are culled in order to prevent the alleged spread of tick-borne diseases to Red Grouse, even though there is no scientific evidence to support this. In arid regions of the southern USA, overgrazing has left the terrain vulnerable to wildfires, which have swept across vast areas, depleting them of jackrabbits – another eagle staple.

Crash course

In addition to transforming the eagle's landscape, we have littered it with hazardous obstacles. Power lines kill many eagles, through collision or electrocution. The latter occurs on poles where eagles can touch two wires simultaneously. These accidents, like others, are most prevalent among wandering, inexperienced young eagles. They are rare in the UK but more common in flat landscapes elsewhere, where power lines offer convenient perches in the absence of trees. In July 2009, the American energy company PacifiCorp was prosecuted for having caused the deaths of 232 Golden Eagles since January 2007. Other eagle species are also hit hard: in some areas of the Russian steppes an estimated 15 dead Steppe Eagles (a close relative of the Golden Eagle) are retrieved along every 10km (6 miles) of power line.

The recent proliferation of wind farms also poses a threat to all large raptors, including both our eagle species. Those huge blades revolve with deceptive speed – often too fast for a passing raptor to take evasive action. So far this has not proved a major cause of mortality in the UK. However, in 2008 a proposal was rejected to build 181 wind turbines on the island of Lewis because of the potential hazard to rare birds, including eagles, and in 2014 a White-tailed Eagle was found dead at the foot of a wind turbine in Tayside. Elsewhere the situation is more serious: numerous White-tailed Eagles have died at wind farms in Norway, and it is estimated that some 70 Golden Eagles every year fall victim to this hazard in central-west California, USA.

Traffic can also pose a problem, with young eagles of both species sometimes struck by cars while feeding on roadside carrion. In Germany it is not uncommon for White-tailed Eagles to be killed by trains when scavenging from animals like Roe Deer that are left on the tracks. There are even records of Golden Eagles killed by low-flying jets and, in one case, by a glider that the bird attacked as a territorial interloper.

Below: A Wedge-tailed Eagle killed by traffic while feeding on the ground beside an Australian highway. All large eagle species are vulnerable to such accidents.

Pollution

Pesticides and other pollutants poison the landscape for many raptors. Species that feed primarily on fish and/or birds, including White-tailed Eagles, are the worst hit. Toxins accumulate in the soil or water and work their way up the food chain to the eagles by a process known as bioaccumulation. DDT, an insecticide used widely on crops after the Second World War, had a catastrophic effect on species such as Peregrine Falcons and Bald Eagles, thinning their eggshells and thus causing breeding failure. The organochoride dieldrin, used in sheep dips and ingested by the raptors when scavenging carcasses, had a similar effect. Both products have long been banned in the UK. Golden Eagles, which feed on a higher proportion of mammals, are less vulnerable than White-tailed Eagles to this kind of pollution, although not immune to it.

Above: Bald Eagles in the USA suffered catastrophic breeding failures during the 1960s and 1970s as a result of DDT.

Heavy metals are also deadly. Lead poisoning is a prime cause of death for White-tailed Eagles in Germany. The birds ingest the lead when feeding on the carcasses of deer, boar or waterfowl that have been peppered with lead shot but escaped the hunters to die elsewhere. Similar problems have been found in the United States, where Golden Eagles feed on jackrabbits.

Right: White-tailed Eagles may ingest lead when feeding on the carcasses of animals shot by hunters.

Disturbance

Eagles – especially Golden Eagles – are shy nesters and easily disturbed. Adults spooked by noise or intrusion may leave the nest for up to two hours, time enough for a predator to nip in and grab the eggs or nestlings. Studies in Scotland have shown that breeding success correlates with nest disturbance, with human intrusion of more than 750m (2,460ft) from a nest being enough to alarm adults, and that eyries situated close to areas of human activity are the least used.

Disturbance can take such noisy forms as road construction, mining or foresty work. However, it can also arise from leisure activities such as hill walking and rock climbing. Studies in Norway have shown that the Easter holidays, when many people hit the slopes to ski, have an impact on breeding success in Golden Eagles. Such activities have become more popular in recent times with, for example, record numbers of hill walkers taking to the Cairngorms. They have arisen alongside the popularity of ecotourism – involving people who actively wish to see wildlife such as eagles – and scientists must balance concerns about disturbance with the many benefits ecotourism brings. Compromises include signs warning people away from nest-sites during the breeding season, designated watch points from which to view eagles from a safe distance, and – since 2015 – a 'traffic light' system of warning colours to advise rock climbers when they are encroaching on the breeding territory of a rare raptor.

Above: Hikers in the Scottish Highlands may disturb nesting eagles if they wander too close to nest sites. However, most eyries are located well away from trails.

Targeted

Most of the harm caused by humans described thus far is unintended: the eagles are the unfortunate casualties of the demands our species places on the natural environment. Unfortunately, it does not stop there. The Industrial Revolution, which brought firearms and industrial poisons, plus a newly commercial dimension to farming and sport hunting, skewed the respect that we once had for these birds.

Above: Grouse shooting is an important commercial activity in the Scottish Highlands, and Golden Eagles in some regions are still illegally persecuted for their predation on game birds.

Landowners began to see them as competitors – thieves of game birds and livestock – and, for the first time, they became the targets of direct aggression. Although livestock losses to eagles are negligible (see page 60), and are far outweighed in commercial terms by the many other ways in which free-ranging stock comes to harm, and although the killing of eagles has long been illegal around the world, the practice continues to this day.

Here in Britain a handful of illegal killings is still reported every year (see page 97), and many more almost certainly go unreported. Scientists believe that this persecution is the single biggest inhibiting factor behind the further recovery of both our eagle species. It is not only a tragedy for the individual birds but can also have broader repercussions. In Scotland, for example, most recorded Golden Eagle killings occur in the Eastern Highlands, causing birds from the Western Highlands to move across and take over the vacant territories.

In Britain the killing began in earnest in the early 19th century, when estate managers first started paying gamekeepers to get rid of eagles and other raptors, and continued unabated into the early 20th century. The numbers make grim reading: records from one estate in the Cairngorms show 295 eagles killed between 1820 and 1826. The two World Wars, during which many estates went largely unmanaged, brought some respite. By this time, however, the White-tailed Eagle had already been driven to extinction and the Golden Eagle was fast heading the same way. The problem has diminished since killing eagles became illegal in 1954, but it has not gone away.

Elsewhere things are even worse. The survey of 266 Golden Eagles that died in Spain from 1980 to 1990 (see page 88) concluded that 67 per cent had been shot, trapped or poisoned. In the United States an estimated 20,000 Golden Eagles were killed from the mid-1930s to 1963, when the species was first granted state protection. Most were shot from light aircraft, with at least 1,000 being killed every year in Texas alone in 1942–1947. This staggering figure represents the most prolific state-sponsored destruction of Golden Eagles anywhere and was driven by a bounty placed on the birds' heads.

The killing takes various forms. Shooting was once the most popular. With eagles now legally protected, however, and the sound of a gunshot a dead give-away, subtler methods are often preferred. Trapping is one – sometimes in inhumane leghold traps, in which the bird has its legs crushed

Above: A stuffed Golden Eagle, looking rather tattier and less magnificent than the living version.

and is left to die in agony. Eagles may also die in traps set for other 'problem' animals, such as crows, starving to death before anybody returns to check the trap. Some such deaths may be less accidental than presumed.

The most insidious method of killing eagles is poisoning, usually by setting bait such as a Rabbit, laced with a lethal toxin such as the banned insecticide carbofuran. This illegal practice takes an annual toll of carrion-eating raptors across the UK, especially in Scotland, including Buzzards, Red Kites and eagles. The targets may often ostensibly be other 'problem' birds, such as crows, but the poison does not discriminate. The bird may fly some distance from the site before it succumbs, so often the body is never found.

Elsewhere in the world, poisoned bait intended for other predators – including, in America, Wolves and Coyotes – finds its way into eagles. Secondary poisoning, when eagles consume prey that has consumed poison,

Above: Traps set for crows often capture birds of prey, including eagles.

also takes a toll: Golden Eagles in California have died after eating California Ground Squirrels that have ingested the rodenticide chlorophacinone.

It is not only adult eagles that are illegally persecuted. Both UK species were once also popular targets for egg collectors. This once legal pastime declined in popularity in the UK after the Second World War, and became a crime with the passing of the Wildlife and Countryside Act of 1981. Nonetheless, today the birds remain potential targets for a small band of dedicated collectors who prize the eggs of rare species most highly. Conservationists keep watch over occupied eyries, where possible, but from 1997-2000 four White-tailed Eagle clutches were lost from the Isle of Mull. In some regions, including China, live Golden Eagles are also captured for falconry (see page 105) – usually as eggs, which are raised in an incubator or as hatchlings.

Below: This Victorian museum collection of British bird eggs includes those of several rare species.

Scotland's eagle shame

The illegal killing of eagles and other raptors continues in Scotland today, despite having been illegal across the UK since the Protection of Birds Act of 1954. The period 1980–2009 saw 51 verified cases of Golden Eagles poisoned and 27 shot or trapped. These cases are almost certainly just the tip of the iceberg. The great majority took place on land managed as grouse moors, where land managers resent the eagles as a threat to commercial Red Grouse shooting.

In recent times the tide of opinion has turned. A well-publicised case from Peeblesshire in August 2007, when a female Golden Eagle from the only breeding pair in the Borders was found poisoned, provoked public outrage – notably among members of the Scottish Parliament – and prompted a review of wildlife crime policy.

The penalties for criminals have since been stiffened: in January 2015, gamekeeper George Mutch became the first person to be imprisoned for raptor persecution (on four counts relating to Goshawks and other raptors). Nonetheless, the problem persists. An RSPB report, *The Illegal Killing of Birds of Prey in Scotland 2012*, reported three Golden Eagles killed that year, one shot, one trapped and one poisoned.

'We applaud the continued focus on tackling raptor persecution by the Scottish Government, but much remains to be done,' said Stuart Housden, RSPB Scotland director. 'The deaths of these Golden Eagles are particularly appalling, given that the Golden Eagle was recently voted the nation's favourite species in the SNH poll for the Year of Natural Scotland. These crimes have no place in 21st century Scotland, and responsible land managers must make that clear to all partners.'

Right: This poisoned Golden Eagle, held by RSPB Scotland Head of Investigations Bob Elliot, was discovered by walkers in Glen Orchy, 2009.

Eagles in Culture

Iconic – it's a modern marketing cliché, but if there is one animal that warrants the adjective, it is surely the eagle. Only in the last couple of centuries have we come to regard these birds as threats and competitors. Before then, in awe of their strength and powers of flight, our attitude was generally one of reverence. Indeed, from the start of recorded history eagles have appeared as icons and emblems, embodying such virtues as freedom and nobility. They have worked their way into everything from religious ceremony and military regalia to poetry and pop music, and to this day pervade our culture. It is the Golden Eagle more than any other species that has attracted this attention, but the White-tailed Eagle also has its place.

Pride, power and politics

The idealised qualities of the eagle – power, pride, courage, freedom and so on – make it the perfect national emblem. Its pleasing shape also helps. The Golden Eagle itself is the national bird of Albania, Afghanistan, Egypt, Germany and Mexico, and in 2013 a parliamentary motion was proposed to anoint it the national bird of Scotland. Other countries that celebrate eagles of one kind or another as their national bird include Indonesia (Javan Hawk Eagle), Panama (Harpy Eagle), Spain (Spanish Imperial Eagle), the United States (Bald Eagle) and Zambia (African Fish Eagle).

Eagles – often explicitly the Golden Eagle – also occur as motifs in the coats of arms of at least 29 countries, including Armenia, Ghana, Palestine, Romania and Yemen. The White-tailed Eagle appears less often, although it is thought to be the white bird depicted on the Polish and Serbian coats of arms. Generally it is shown grasping a fish (usually a pike) in its talons, to distinguish it from the Golden Eagle. In heraldry the Golden Eagle is celebrated

Above: Coat of arms featuring an eagle, above the main entrance of the University of Warsaw, Poland.

Opposite: A traditional eagle hunter of central Asia holds his Golden Eagle aloft in a pose that emphasises the bird's power and majesty.

Above: Engraving from 1874 of Roman soldiers bearing the Aquila standard, based on figures from the Arch of Constantine.

Below: A German *stahlhelm* helmet from WWII displays an eagle clutching a swastika.

as the 'king of birds' – the equivalent of the Lion as 'king of beasts'. Eagles in heraldry are generally 'displayed', with wings and legs extended, but may also appear as 'close' (perched) or 'rising' (taking off).

Leaders throughout history, from the Persians and Ancient Egyptians to the Austro-Hungarians and Ottomans, have drawn upon the eagle in one form or another as a symbol of their power. Napoleon Bonaparte – never one for understatement – chose for his arms an eagle perched on a thunderbolt. Most influential was undoubtedly the Holy Roman Empire (27 BC–AD 395), whose legions swept across Europe, and south to North Africa and the Byzantine Empire, bearing the Aquila as their standard. The honour of carrying the eagle went to an *aquilifer*, or eagle bearer, whose job held huge military significance. A lost standard meant disgrace and military disaster, and the army would go to great lengths both to protect a standard and recover a lost one. As the Roman Empire split into east and west, so the eagle was depicted with two heads, one representing each division.

The success of the Roman Empire has spurred many other powers to appropriate the eagle as a symbol. The United States government adopted the Bald Eagle – along with such other Roman conventions as the senate. In Germanic nations, eagles have served as emblems from Charlemagne to the Weimar Republic (1919–1933).

Most notoriously, they were adopted by the Nazis, and the image of an eagle clutching a swastika in its talons is one of the more chilling manifestations of humanity's obsession with the bird's power (not that we should blame the eagle). In Arab culture, the eagle was the personal symbol of Saladin and appeared as a coat of arms in nationalist movements in Egypt, Iraq, Palestine and Syria.

Myth and religion

Left: Mosaic depicting the Greek god Zeus taking the form of an eagle in order to kidnap the youth Ganymede.

Eagles have held a spiritual significance in cultures from ancient times, often acting as intercessionaries between humankind on Earth and deities up above. In the Hellenistic tradition of Ancient Greece, an eagle was the totem of Zeus, who took the bird's form when swooping down to carry off Ganymede to Mount Olympus. In Ancient Rome an eagle was, in addition to its military prestige, revered as both the incarnation and the messenger of the sky god Jupiter; when an emperor died and was cremated, an eagle was released into the flames to carry the soul up to heaven. In ancient Norse mythology an eagle sat atop Yggdrasil, the giant tree of life that ran through the universe.

Celtic mythology hailed the eagle as the oldest animal in the world. It acted as an oracle, giving advice and foretelling an army's fortunes in battle (a high-soaring eagle meant victory). Celtic myths generally relate to the White-tailed Eagle, however, which was associated with warfare from its habit of scavenging corpses

Above: Eagle pulpit in Reims cathedral, France.

on a battlefield. Indeed, achaeological evidence suggests that the Celts left out their dead to be consumed by eagles – as, until recent times, members of the Parsi Zoroastrian tradition in India left out their dead for vultures in 'towers of silence'. These myths are known largely from Wales, where the Celtic name for Snowdonia, Eyyri, means the place of the eagle. Scotland offers less evidence, although prehistoric tombs found on Orkney containing the bones of White-tailed Eagles further confirm the importance of this species in funeral rites.

The Bible contains scattered references to eagles, sometimes as carrion eaters but also as messengers of God (Revelations 8:13) and as a symbol of protection – as when representing God carrying the ancient Israelites out of slavery in Egypt (Exodus 19:4). In the Anglican tradition an eagle commonly appears carved into a pulpit, supporting the Bible, its spread wings symbolising the spread of Christianity around the world.

In Hindu tradition the eagle figure Garuda is the mount of the god Vishnu. So huge that it reputedly blocked out the sun, this lesser divinity is depicted with the body of a man and the beak of an eagle. Today it gives its name to the national airline of Indonesia. Further east, in Japanese myth the eagle takes the form of the Tengu, a half-bird/half-human monster that acts as protector of the mountains and controller of the weather, and performs mischievous acts of revenge on human intruders.

Below: Sculpture in Bangkok, Thailand, depicting the eagle figure Garuda from Hindu tradition.

Eagles in Native American culture

Nowhere in the world has the eagle – and specifically the Golden Eagle – enjoyed greater spiritual significance than among the native peoples of North America. Many tribes, especially those of the Great Plains and the south-west, including the Apache, Cherokee, Cheyenne, Blackfoot and Navaho, revered this bird as a sacred representative of the Great Spirit. It played a pivotal role in the spiritual life of the community, being celebrated through rituals such as the Sioux eagle dance. In the words of Thomas E. Mails, a renowned authority on Native American history and culture:

The male Golden Eagle flew above all the creatures of the world and saw everything. Nothing matched his courage and his swiftness, and his talons had the strength of a giant's hand. The eagle was very holy. He was the solar or sun bird, and his feathers were regarded as the rays of the sun.
(Mails 1991)

Eagle feathers had a particular symbolic power among these cultures – one that has been likened to that of a crucifix for Christians. They were used to adorn medicine pipes, doctor's rattles and prayer sticks. Most importantly, they were bestowed upon warriors who had proved their bravery in battle – with one feather earned by one 'coup', an action such as the landing of a blow on an enemy. The favoured feathers were the black-and-white tail feathers of subadult Golden Eagles. The spectacular headdresses, or war bonnets, worn by senior warriors comprised some 60 feathers and required at least five eagles.

To obtain these feathers without damaging the birds' spiritual powers, eagles were caught by hand. A warrior would crouch in a pit beneath a camouflaged tarpaulin,

Above: 1940s image depicting Native American warrior of the Sioux tribe wearing eagle headdress.

Above: Former NASA astronaut Commander John Herrington presents the eagle staff during the opening ceremony of the American Indian Science and Engineering Society National Conference at the Oregon Convention Centre.

upon which bait would be set. When the bird landed, the warrior would reach up through a hole and grab it by its legs, dragging it in and killing it. This hazardous practice could result in severe injury for the warrior. Incense was burned and prayers offered to appease the Great Spirit. The Hopi people would capture eagles as nestlings – just one from a nest – and raise them by hand until the feathers grew and could be harvested.

Today eagles are still held to be sacred in Native American communities, and the custom of awarding feathers has extended to such contemporary rituals as high-school graduation. It is sometimes difficult for the authorities to strike a balance between Federal Conservation Law and Native American spiritual freedoms. In 1978, the American Indian Religious Freedom Act granted tribal communities the power to perform rituals and possess sacred objects. Under this law, legally certified Native Americans may acquire a licence to obtain eagle feathers legally for spiritual or religious reasons. The US National Eagle Repository preserves dead birds – recovered from accidental or illegal killings – from which such feathers are dispensed. The penalties for killing an eagle, or for possessing feathers without a licence, are severe. Nonetheless a black market in feathers thrives, with many of the feathers coming from birds poached in Canada.

Eagle words

The English word 'eagle' comes, via the French *aigle*, from the Latin *aquila*. In Ancient Rome the *aquila* was the military standard borne by a legion (see page 100). This word, in turn, is thought to derive from either *aquilus*, meaning dark and swarthy, or *aquilo*, meaning wind. Until the 1760s, it was used in English only for the Golden Eagle. The White-tailed Eagle was known as *erne*, derived, via Old English, from the Old Norse *örn*.

In the birds' scientific names, *chrysaetos* (*Aquila chrysaetos*) is derived from the Ancient Greek χρυσάετος, meaning 'golden', and *albicilla* (*Haliaeetus albicilla*) is Latin for 'white

tailed'. Today the association of the Golden Eagle with power and nobility is reflected in its common name across many other languages. In French, for example, the Golden Eagle is *Aigle royal*, and in Spanish *Águila real*, both of which mean 'royal eagle'.

Not only are eagles prominent in the English language, embodied in such metaphors as 'eagle-eyed', they are also a part of our very alphabet. Our lower-case letter 'a' is thought to derive from the stylised image of a perched eagle, via Ancient Egyptian hieroglyphs and the Phoenician alphabet.

Eagles in falconry

Perhaps the ultimate expression of our admiration for eagles has been our attempt to harness their powers to our own ends. Falconry – the hunting of live prey using trained falcons and other birds of prey – has its origins in Central Asia and dates back to at least 2000 BC. It probably arrived in Europe with the invading Huns and Alans in around AD 400. In medieval times falconry became a popular sport and status symbol among the nobility, with King Harold of England being depicted in the Bayeux Tapestry (1070s) carrying a hawk on his wrist. By the late 18th and 19th centuries, with the advent of firearms as the hunting tool of choice, falconry fell into decline, although a revival in the late 19th and early 20th centuries saw a number of falconry books published and the introduction of the sport to North America.

Above: King Harold depicted in the Bayeux Tapestry bearing a falcon on his wrist.

Above: Falcons, such as this Saker Falcon, have traditionally been the preferred birds for falconry.

The eagle has long carried great prestige in falconry. The celebrated *Book of St Albans* (*Boke of St Albans*), first printed in 1486, provides a hierarchy of birds of prey, showing the social rank for which each species is appropriate. An eagle sits at the very top, its use reserved for emperors, while a kestrel languishes at the bottom, deemed suitable only for knaves.

Certainly the eagle – and again, it is primarily the Golden Eagle we are talking about here – can be trained as a highly effective hunter, able to take larger prey than any other raptor. However, its size, strength and aggression introduces practical problems for the falconer. In Europe it was a bird kept more for prestige than hunting, with no record until the mid-19th century of any attempt to train one. Similarly, hunting with Golden Eagles has never caught on in the United States, where smaller species such as Ferruginous and Harris Hawks are preferred. Indeed, falconers fear the great raptor as a predator of such smaller birds, and keep a close watch on the skies when in eagle country. The White-tailed Eagle has never been trained as a hunter's bird in falconry, although you may sometimes see captive birds flown in falconry displays.

Alan Gates, a falconer from Jersey, has written extensively about training and hunting with Golden Eagles. He explains that for a long time the practice of hunting with eagles in Europe was hampered by mistakenly pursuing the same training methods as those used for smaller raptors, such as Goshawks. This generally resulted in bored, uncooperative eagles and injured falconers, and gave the bird a bad reputation. Gates's own accounts of training eagles to hunt rabbits and hares, using methods that cater for the birds' great intelligence and power – and need for greater space – make fascinating reading. They also emphasise the thrill of the pursuit:

Above: Falconer Alan Gates with one of his trained Golden Eagles.

The stoop of a Golden Eagle from 1,000 feet or more is an event one rarely forgets. As the large bird folds into the teardrop stoop one senses an excitement as this silent natural missile plummets earthwards. Neck craning skywards, you are aware that you have momentarily stopped breathing, and the rhythmic beating of your heart sounding in your head is being assaulted by a ripping sound as the stooping eagle nears four hundred feet from the earth. The velocity of this feathered missile seems to have greatly increased as the air screams through the slit in the single leg bell. At one hundred feet the eagle starts to level out of the stoop. Cutting across the top of the heather-clad hill at about ten feet, she closes in on a fleeing hill hare.

Hunting with eagles in Central Asia

Europeans may have found it hard to train Golden Eagles. However, in the central steppes of Asia, where falconry originated, there is a dedicated band of hunters who pursue the sport to this day. The practice takes place among the Kazakh and Kyrgyz people in the Tien Shan mountains of southern Kazakhstan, extending into Turkistan and Western Mongolia. Known as *berkutchy* in Kazakh, it has ancient roots among the nomadic Khitan dynasty, which conquered part of northern China in AD 936–45.

Today there are some 250 eagle hunters. For these individuals, who have each inherited the tradition from their father, it involves a lifetime's dedication. Their relationship with the eagle is all-consuming, the hunter going without sleep for long periods during the training and keeping the bird unsighted under a hood until its dependence upon him becomes complete. Bonds between a hunter and his eagle may last for more than 20 years. The main quarry is the Corsac Fox – a small fox of the Asian steppes – and one experienced eagle may take

Below: A procession of Kazakh Golden Eagle hunters in the Altai Mountains, Western Mongolia.

up to 40 foxes per season. However, the birds are also flown at Roe Deer and Goitered Gazelles. Sometimes, amazingly, they are even flown at Wolves, which – although the smaller Asiatic race – are nonetheless formidable adversaries and well capable of killing an eagle if they can get their teeth into it.

Most hunting takes place during winter, when snow makes the quarry easiest to see. The hunter takes his bird out by horseback to a high vantage point, holding it on his right wrist (by contrast with the left wrist used in other forms of falconry), and using a special wooden brace to help support the bird's great weight. He releases it when a fox is sighted. The eagle swoops low and strikes the fox on the back of the neck, pulling it to the ground instantly or 'riding' it until the animal collapses. Sometimes the eagle kills its quarry outright; at other times the hunter arrives on horseback to dispatch it. The eagle is then lured off its prey with a piece of meat as a reward. An annual Golden Eagle Festival is held in the first weekend of October: up to 50 hunters compete for a variety of prizes, awarded for speed, agility and accuracy.

Above: A Kazakh Golden Eagle hunter atop his horse.

Below: Clad in a fox fur coat, Kazakh golden eagle hunter Sailau Jadik allows his eagle to spread its wings.

Man-eaters?

Above: A Crowned Eagle in Zimbabwe with its Vervet Monkey kill. This species may sometimes have preyed on early hominids.

Perhaps the ultimate expression of our respect for eagles as predators is the fear that we ourselves might fall victim to their talons. This idea has appeared in mythology since ancient times and has spawned numerous sensational stories over the years. Many – including at least one from Scotland – involve Golden Eagles, but none of these has ever been verified. You should certainly not trust a 2014 YouTube video, in which a Golden Eagle appears to snatch a toddler from a Montreal park: this was quickly revealed as a student hoax – but not before it went viral.

One tale that has long divided opinion involves a White-tailed Eagle in Norway. On the afternoon of 5 June 1932, this bird reputedly snatched three-and-half-year-old Svanhild Hartvigsen from her home and deposited her unharmed on a mountain ledge below its eyrie. Svanhild died in 2010, aged 81 years, but was never able to remember anything of the incident.

Eagles do occasionally attack people. They have even launched aerial assaults on paragliders. But such incidents result from territorial aggression and are not the same thing as predation. Certainly a Golden or White-tailed Eagle is capable, in principle, of killing a small child. But the difficulty with such stories generally concerns the birds' ability to lift anything that heavy; Svanhild Hartvigsen is thought to have weighed 19kg when allegedly snatched, at least three times the usual maximum load for a White-tailed Eagle.

The most reliable stories of eagles preying on humans involve the Crowned Eagle of Africa. This powerful forest species regularly takes monkeys the size of a human infant. In one authenticated case, a seven-year-old boy was ambushed and severely injured. In another, a child's skull was found in a Crowned Eagle nest. Perhaps our smaller ancestors had more to fear than we do: piercings in the skull of the Taung Child, a famous fossil of the prehistoric hominid *Australopithecus africanus*, unearthed in South Africa, were found to be the talon marks of an eagle; a Crowned Eagle was the most likely culprit.

From pop to poetry

For centuries the ideas and images of eagles have adorned Western culture in one form or another. We have driven in eagle cars (the Chrysler Corporation's Eagle Talon and Eagle Premier), we have flown in Eagle aircraft (the Cessna 421 Golden Eagle), we have hit eagles in golf (if we are lucky), and we have gone to watch Eagles play football (Crystal Palace FC) and American football (Philadelphia Eagles). At the cinema we have watched Richard Burton in *Where Eagles Dare* (Brian G. Hutton 1968) and Robert Redford in *Legal Eagles* (Ivan Reitman 1990). We have read about eagles in Tolkein and Shakespeare, and have sung along to 'Eagle' (Abba), 'Fly Like an Eagle' (Steve Miller Band), 'On the Wings of an Eagle' (John Denver) and, of course, almost anything by The Eagles.

Above: A theatrical release poster for *The Eagle Has Landed*, 1976.

But there is surely no finer expression of our fascination with eagles than the short poem 'The Eagle (Fragment)', by Alfred, Lord Tennyson (1809–1892), first published in 1851. These two short stanzas, which make a nod in their reverence for nature to the earlier era of the romantic poets, undoubtedly refer to a Golden Eagle and were inspired by the Poet Laureate's visits to the Spanish Pyrenees (the 'wrinkled sea' is poetic licence). Impressive in literary terms for its powerful alliteration, rhythm and symbolism, the poem also conveys obvious personal experience. Tennyson's eagle is no eagle of the imagination.

Above: Collection of original 1950s *Eagle* comics, featuring Dan Dare.

He clasps the crag with crooked hands;
Close to the sun in lonely lands,
Ring'd with the azure world, he stands.

The wrinkled sea beneath him crawls;
He watches from his mountain walls,
And like a thunderbolt he falls.

Understanding, Protecting and Enjoying Eagles

Attitudes towards eagles are changing. Science and conservation now allow us to see beyond the birds' traditional roles – as either iconic hero or lamb-killing villain – and to recognise their importance in the natural world. The more we learn about these birds, the better we are able to address the threats they face and find ways in which to get along with them. Across Europe, dedicated conservation – including some innovative reintroduction programmes – has helped to arrest the decline of eagles in many places. Meanwhile, our appetite for seeing these magnificent raptors in the wild is stronger than ever.

Finding out

Research into eagles has moved on from the days when scientists spent days perched on perilous crags in appalling weather hoping for a glimpse of the birds. Today's technology enables us to probe deeply into the lives of these birds and understand how human activities impact upon them.

In the USA, for example, scientists are studying the Golden Eagle population east of the Mississippi by means of cellular GPS-GSM transmitters, which track individual birds throughout the year in order to establish what hazards they face along their flyways. The eagles are trapped using rocket nets at sites baited with road-killed deer, then each outfitted with a GSM telemetry unit affixed to a backpack harness. The devices collect data at 15-minute intervals all year round. The researchers can use this to calculate the size of individual winter home ranges and breeding territories, and work out how the

Above: Scientists measure the length of a Golden Eagle's talons. Biometric data is vital in our understanding of these birds.

Opposite: Scientists measure and weigh two Golden Eagle chicks at a remote nest site in the Scottish Highlands during the 2015 National Golden Eagle Survey, conducted by the RSPB and Scottish Natural Heritage.

Above: Conservationist Justin Grant attaches GPS satellite tags to a Golden Eagle chick at its nest in the Scottish Highlands.

birds use their habitats. Similar projects in the western USA have provided vital information in the planning of wind farms, enabling energy companies to avoid locating their facilities in key eagle migration corridors.

In the UK, an initiative called Raptortrack is tracking individual Golden Eagles in the Cairngorms National Park, fitting satellite tags to young birds at the nest to study their behaviour and movements. The lives of these individual birds now play out online (see page 124), with each given a regular blog and updated map. White-tailed Eagles, similarly, have been the subject of intensive research ever since their reintroduction in 1975, with the birds' movements monitored using coloured wing tags, leg rings and radio transmitters, and their dietary habits revealed through analysis of prey remains at the nest.

Monitoring numbers is also vital. In 2015 there was a new six-month survey of Scotland's Golden Eagles. Funded by the RSPB and Scottish Natural Heritage, this was the first such survey since 2003. Its results should allow researchers to find out what effect conservation efforts have had on the population.

Eagle conservation

Both the Golden and White-tailed Eagle are protected in Britain today under Schedule 1 of the Wildlife and Countryside Act 1981. This states that it is an offence to intentionally take, injure or kill the birds, and to take, damage or destroy their nests, eggs or young. It is also an offence to intentionally or recklessly disturb them near their nests during the breeding season. Violation can mean a £5,000 fine and/or a prison sentence of up to six months.

Meanwhile the RSPB and other conservation groups are giving eagles a helping hand. Their work aims to reduce persecution, secure safe habitats, involve local communities, and lobby government, landowners and other key decision makers to keep the birds' welfare on the agenda.

Golden Eagle

The International Union for Conservation of Nature (IUCN) classes the Golden Eagle as of 'Least Concern' because it is not currently threatened with extinction on a worldwide basis. Nonetheless, populations in many countries remain under threat and continued conservation is thus a necessity.

Above: A police notice alerts the public to the importance of protecting eagles from criminal persecution.

Below: The restoration of native Caledonian pine forest in the Scottish Highlands will provide Golden Eagles with important habitat.

UNDERSTANDING, PROTECTING AND ENJOYING EAGLES

Above: A Golden Eagle perches on a power line in the USA. Simple modifications can make these lines safe for any large birds that perch on them.

In the UK the species has been slowly recovering since the outlawing of hunting and the banning of harmful pesticides in the last century. There is, however, a need for further action. While populations in western Scotland are faring well, large swathes of suitable habitat in the central and eastern Highlands – once Golden Eagle strongholds – remain unoccupied. This suggests that there is still a problem in these areas. Ongoing conservation measures range from educating mountain climbers in preventing nest disturbance, to replanting native Caledonian pine forests to improve habitat.

In the USA, meanwhile, industrial companies working in Golden Eagle areas have commissioned research in order to understand and minimise any harmful effects of their own activities. There has also been significant progress in reducing the number of eagles killed by electrocution and wire collisions. Relatively small changes can make a big difference: on power lines in the USA, for example, raising the central insulator more than 1m above the cross-arm and positioning the ground-wire at a lower height have reduced the incidence of Golden Eagles striking the wires with their wings. Golden Eagles could be safe from electrocution everywhere if all power lines were modified in this way.

White-tailed Eagle

The White-tailed Eagle, due to its broad distribution and slowly recovering population, is also classed by the IUCN as 'of Least Concern'. In the UK, however, it is Red-Listed, with a population of no more than 100 pairs. Here, as in most European countries, it remains a conversation priority.

The decline of the White-tailed Eagle across Europe began in the early nineteenth century and led to extinction in many counties, including the UK. Protection began in the 1970s, although the impact of mercury and pesticide poisoning continued to reduce breeding success into the 1980s. Since then, the population has recovered steadily, enabling the species to recolonise several former breeding areas – including the Netherlands, where in 2006 it returned of its own accord to breed for the first time in decades.

Studies from northern and central Europe have shown that this growing population still has a broad genetic diversity. Thus the risk of inbreeding is low and the bird's future prospects are good. The recovery of this once endangered species is a true conservation success story. However, significant threats remain, ranging from illegal persecution in Scotland to wind turbine collisions in Norway, so conservationists are allowing no room for complacency.

Bringing eagles back home

Disappearing eagles need not disappear forever. Conservationists have managed to reintroduce the White-tailed Eagle to Scotland after more than 50 years of extinction. This pioneering project has seen many ups and downs, but its success has paved the way for similar reintroductions elsewhere, both of White-tailed Eagles and of other birds of prey – including Golden Eagles.

Scottish sea eagle returns

The first attempt to reintroduce White-tailed Eagles to Scotland was in 1959, when an adult and two juveniles from Norway were released at Glen Etive, Argyll. In 1968 the RSPB released another four Norwegian eaglets on Fair Isle. Neither attempt succeeded, with the numbers now thought to have been too low. One bird developed a taste for chickens and was recaptured; others are thought to have fallen victim to oiling by Fulmars (see page 87).

In 1975, the Nature Conservancy Council (now Scottish Natural Heritage) launched a longer-term reintroduction project on Rum, a craggy island in the Inner Hebrides where the eagles had bred

Below: RSPB staff member Claire Smith holds a White-tailed Eagle chick, newly arrived from Norway for the East Scotland Sea Eagle reintroduction project, June 2011.

until 1907. Over the next decade, 82 eaglets were imported from nests in Norway and, once they could fly, released on the island. Despite the lack of parental guidance, the birds thrived and soon began to expand their range to neighbouring islands. The first successful breeding took place in 1985 on Mull, which has subsequently become a stronghold (see page 121). More pairs have nested in every year since, gradually rebuilding the population.

As back-up, Scottish Natural Heritage and the RSPB undertook a follow-up programme in Wester Ross on the nearby Scottish mainland, where from 1993 to 1998 they released 58 young eagles. This release proved equally successful, and birds from both reintroductions have since continued to expand their range along the Scottish west coast. The turn of the millennium, in 2000, saw the 100th wild chick fledged from this re-established population.

To help broaden the gene pool and allow the species to regain its full former range, a third reintroduction took place in Fife, on the east coast. The birds were released over a five-year period from 2007. This release has also proved successful, with the first pair breeding in 2013. Thus the White-tailed Eagle is now fully re-established as a breeding bird in the UK. In 2015 the number of breeding pairs topped 100 for the first time.

Reintroductions in Ireland

Reintroduction is now also under way in Ireland, for both species. The White-tailed Eagle last bred in 1912 in County Mayo. In 2007, a first batch of eaglets was released into Killarney National Park in the south-west, and by 2015 there were 13 territorial pairs across Ireland. Meanwhile, the Golden Eagle, which became extinct in Ireland nearly a century ago, is being reintroduced to the north-west, where research suggests that there is enough suitable prey and habitat to support up to 100 pairs.

The long-term success of both programmes will depend upon local goodwill and support, especially among the farming and fishing communities. The Golden Eagle Trust, which is running the project in collaboration with the RSPB and other partners, is working closely with these communities.

Above: A sign in Norfolk, England, objecting to the proposed reintroduction of White-tailed Eagles to the county.

Watching Eagles

There are few things more exciting for any British wildlife lover than watching a wild eagle. Thankfully this thrill is readily available, provided you are willing to make the effort. For those in the south, this means a long journey up to the Scottish Highlands – and, once up there, it may mean pulling on your boots and hitting the hills.

The Golden Eagle is much the more numerous and widely distributed of our two eagle species. However, it is more wary of people and tends to frequent more remote areas. By contrast, its White-tailed cousin may be less numerous, but it offers more predictable sightings – often in places that are easier to get to than those inhabited by the Golden Eagle.

Golden Eagles

Golden Eagles occur throughout north-west Scotland, including on the Outer and Inner Hebrides. Smaller populations occur in the central and eastern Highlands, with a handful in south-west Scotland and the Borders. Top spots include the islands of Lewis and Harris (Outer Hebrides); the islands of Skye and Mull (Inner Hebrides); and the west coast and its mountainous hinterland, from the Ardnamurchon Peninsula north to the Localsh, Torridon, Gairloch and Assynt areas. Around Inverness, the Findhorn Valley and Cairngorms National Park are

Above: When in Golden Eagle country, it pays to spend time scanning ridges with binoculars (left); with luck, you may see one break the skyline (right).

Above: A wandering White-tailed Eagle spotted over marshes in Malden, North Essex, on 12 March 2015. Such sightings in England are very rare.

both good areas. There is also, at the time of writing, one Golden Eagle in the English Lake District (see below).

Golden Eagle sightings cannot be ordered up on demand and, for obvious reasons, known nest-sites are kept secret. By talking to locals and/or searching birdwatching sites on the Internet, however, you can get a pretty good idea of where best to look. Bear in mind that these birds wander very widely, so pretty much anywhere in the Highlands has potential. Your best bet is to visit a promising area and then hit the hills, choosing good weather and scanning the ridges. Allow enough time and you should get lucky.

White-tailed Eagles

Most of Scotland's White-tailed Eagles are found on Mull, Skye and the Outer Hebrides, and on the north-west mainland – notably in the Wester Ross region, between Gairloch and Ullapool. These birds wander widely, as do

England's lonely eagle

Visit Haweswater – a remote reservoir in the eastern Lake District – and you may be lucky enough to catch a glimpse of England's only Golden Eagle. Eddy, as he is affectionately known, lost his mate in 2004 but as of spring 2015 was still performing his annual spring sky dance in the forlorn hope of attracting another. Golden Eagles were once plentiful in the craggy uplands of northern England. Once Eddy has gone, however, the bird will officially be extinct south of the border. Conservationists have ruled out on practical and political grounds any possibility of reintroducing a female. Eddy's best hope is therefore to meet a mate wandering south from the Scottish Borders, where a reintroduction programme is under

way. Meanwhile, to see Eddy for yourself, visit the RSPB watch point at the head of Riggindale Valley (details on RSPB website). Here he is sometimes seen soaring or perched among the craggy outcrops of Kidsty Pike. But, as the local Cumbria Bird Club advises: 'Don't expect him served on a plate!'

Above: Eddy the Eagle soars through Cumbrian skies.

Eagle Island

There is no better place to see eagles in the UK than the Isle of Mull. This is where Scotland's reintroduced White-tailed Eagles first bred and today, with upwards of 16 pairs, the island's population has reached capacity. The BBC's *Springwatch* and *Autumnwatch* series turned these birds into national celebrities, and many thousands of visitors have since enjoyed the public-viewing hides, joined the daily ranger-led trips or followed the RSPB's White-tailed Eagle Trail around the island. In turn, the eagle-watching industry has pumped millions into the local economy, giving a source of pride to the local community and demonstrating to sceptics just how birds of prey can pay their way. Mull also has one of Europe's highest densities of breeding Golden Eagles. These shy birds are, as ever, harder to find than White-tailed Eagles, and tend to stick to the island's rugged interior. Over a few days, however, you have a good chance of seeing both species

Above: Eagles are big news on Mull, with plenty of signs and information to direct the visitor.

– sometimes even in the air simultaneously. Quite apart from eagles, Mull's otters, Red Deer, seals, dolphins and seabirds make this rugged island one of the most rewarding wildlife destinations in Britain.

those from the new east-coast population in Fife, and may turn up almost anywhere around the Scottish coast.

White-tailed Eagles are more tolerant of people than Golden Eagles, and are often seen from boats, harbours and public roads. This has made the species a significant draw in the Western Isles, where it is a highlight of tourist boat trips. In some places, individuals become so habituated to local boats that they can be tempted within easy camera range by a fish tossed off the stern. Some locations, notably Mull, offer designated eagle watchpoints and organised eagle-watching walks.

Elsewhere in Britain, White-tailed Eagles – typically young birds, off course – occasionally wander over from continental Europe, usually turning up on the east coast. They may stick around for a week or so, winding up the local crows and Buzzards, before moving on. As the European population expands, such sightings may become more regular.

In Europe

Across the English Channel or the North Sea there are many other places in which to seek out one or both of our eagle species. Some are easily combined with a family holiday. Here are a few ideas:

- **France** The Alps and Pyrenees both have Golden Eagles, while White-tailed Eagles overwinter on lowland lakes in eastern and central regions.
- **Hungary** White-tailed Eagles breed in small numbers and overwinter in large numbers on fish ponds and wetlands.
- **Norway** White-tailed Eagles have their largest European population here, and are easily seen on a boat trip up the scenic west coast.
- **Spain** Golden Eagles (of the Iberian *homeyeri* race) inhabit mountains across the country – notably the Pyrenees, where numerous other raptors include Griffon Vultures, Lammergeyers and Short-toed Eagles.
- **Sweden** Both species occur in the southern third between Stockholm and Gottenburg; White-tailed Eagles also breed along the Baltic coast.

Below: A White-tailed Eagle soars along the rugged western coast of Norway, where the bird has its largest European population.

Top Tips for Watching Eagles

Above: Great Black-backed Gulls harassing a White-tailed Eagle. The alarm calls of other birds mobbing an eagle often betray its presence.

- Be prepared to walk: eagles – especially Golden Eagles – live in remote areas, often far from roads; the effort makes the reward all the sweeter.
- Scan ridges: eagles are hard to see against a hillside but give themselves away when breaking the skyline. Do it methodically – make a quick scan every time you stop for a breather.
- When scanning a ridge also check prominent perching spots: points where an eagle will get maximum take-off lift from updrafts below.
- Listen out for the anxious calls of crows and Ravens, which are quick to protest at the sight of an eagle and will often mob it in mid-air.
- Take care not to confuse either eagle with the much more common Buzzard (known in Scotland as the 'tourist eagle'). Size can be hard to judge against an empty sky, so look for key identification features (see page 17), such as the length and shape of the wings, head and tail.

- Take a boat trip along the Scottish coast. Such trips provide great opportunities to spot White-tailed Eagles – and sometimes Golden Eagles too. Scan ridges and headlands from the sea.
- Always bring binoculars – it is usually hard to find, let alone identify, an eagle without them. A telescope helps if the bird is perched.
- Take mountain hikes seriously: wear suitable clothing and footwear for upland terrain, and always anticipate a change in the weather; go with a friend or, if alone, tell somebody where you plan to go.
- If you think you may have found an eagle nest-site, keep well away – at least 500m. At known eyries, obey warning signs.
- Use the Internet to research good eagle sites before your trip. Ask around among locals about where eagles have most recently been seen.

Glossary

Afforestation The planting of trees to create a forest (ie: the opposite of deforestation). Often done for commercial purposes but sometimes also in order to regenerate a native habitat for conservation or environmental benefits.

Bioaccumulation The chemical process by which substances, including toxins, are absorbed at a low level of a food chain and pass up as a residue through each link in the chain, with the potential to harm animals at the top – such as eagles.

Cetacean Any member of the whale and dolphin family. There are some 88 species in the order Cetacea, ranging from the UK's diminutive Harbour Porpoise to the enormous Blue Whale, the largest animal that has ever lived.

Contour feathers The small, overlapping feathers that form the surface layer of a bird's plumage – as distinct from the down feathers, which lie underneath, and the flight feathers, which are larger specialised feathers in the wings and tail.

Fingers Birdwatcher's term for the tapered primary wing feathers of eagles and other birds that are visible separately when the wings are spread in soaring flight – thus resembling the fingers of a spread hand.

Flyway A regular route taken by migrating birds, usually being the most efficient means of getting between their breeding and non-breeding quarters. The Nile Valley, for example, is an important flyway for many species that migrate between Africa and Eurasia.

Generalist A bird (or another animal), such as a crow, that is adapted to feed on a variety of food and to find food in different ways - as distinct from a specialist, which relies on its ability to obtain and subsist upon a particular food source (ospreys, for example, catch and eat only fish).

IUCN The International Union for the Conservation of Nature. An international non-governmental organisation founded in 1948 that gathers data in order to monitor the conservation status of all plant and animal species on Earth. The IUCN Red List assigns each species a conservation category, ranging from Least Concern to Critically Endangered.

Kleptoparasite An animal that steals food from another animal that has caught it. Some species, such as the White-tailed Eagle, are opportunist kleptoparasites. Others, such as skuas, depend upon the practice.

Siblicide The deliberate killing of one sibling by another. In some animal species, including the Golden Eagle, this has evolved as a deliberate breeding strategy.

Steppe An ecosystem of temperate regions that comprises wide open grassland with very few trees. The term is usually associated with central Asia, where it is the equivalent of the African savannah or the American prairies.

Taxonomy The science of classification. Taxonomists trace the evolutionary heritage of each organism, determining which can be classified as species, which species make up a genus, which genera form a family and so on.

Terminal band A coloured band, often in black or white, that some birds have across the end of the tail. It is often an important aid to identification.

Theropod A group of swift-moving, carnivorous dinosaurs that first appeared during the Triassic Period (251–199 million years ago) and included such species as Tyrannosaurus Rex. These were the first animals to develop feathers - initially for insulation rather than flight - and were probably the ancestors of birds.

Ungulate Any of a large group of large, hoofed, herbivorous mammals. Some ungulates, such as deer, antelope, sheep, cattle and pigs, are 'even-toed' and have cloven hooves. Others, including horses, rhinos and tapirs, are 'odd-toed' and have either three toes or a single central hoof.

Further Reading and Resources

Books

Crumley, Jim, *The Eagle's Way: Nature's New Frontier in a Northern Landscape* (Kindle Edition)
Interesting and highly readable account of the relationship between Golden Eagles and White-tailed Eagles in Scotland since the reintroduction of the latter, and of the birds' changing relationship with people. An important contribution to the debate about species reintroduction.

Dennis, Roy H (Author) and Campbell, Laurie (Author, Photographer), *Golden Eagles* (Colin Baxter Photography Ltd; New ed., 1997)
An illustrated celebration of the Golden Eagle, describing the life of the bird during each season of the year. It focuses on birds in Scotland and includes extracts from the author's diaries which describe his conservation work. Outstanding images by top Scottish nature photographer Laurie Campbell.

Gordon, Seton Paul, *Days with the Golden Eagle* (Whittles Publishing, first published 1927, new ed, 2003)
Reprint of the classic eagle book from one of the pioneers of nature writing. The author was among the first to observe in detail the daily life of Golden Eagles and to document their habitat, diet and behaviour. Fascinating observations and a compelling narrative.

Tomkies, Mike, *Golden Eagle Years* (Jonathan Cape; 2nd Revised edition, 1994)
Highly readable account from the 1970s of one man's studies of Golden Eagles in the Scottiish Highlands. The author, a former Coldstream Guardsman, is also known for his studies of Scottish Wild Cats. Offers a fascinating insight into the rigours of studying and photographing this elusive bird in remote places and challenging conditions long before the age of satellite telemetry - and of relations with local farmers and landowners.

Love, John A, *A Saga of Sea Eagles* (Whittles Publishing, 2013)
Entertaining and evocative account of the reintroduction of White-tailed Eagles to Scotland, by a key figure in the project since the 1960s. More a memoir than a scientific report, with absorbing insights into the wild places these birds once inhabited and the legends they have spawned.

Watson, Jeff, *The Golden Eagle* (T & AD Poyser, 2nd ed, 2010)
Definitive monograph that first appeared in 1997 and compiled everything known about the Golden Eagle, both in the UK and worldwide. The author, who died before this revision, was one of the world's foremost experts on Golden Eagles. Second edition expanded and updated with much new fascinating information on social interactions and conservation.

Online

A wealth of online resources offers all the information you could possibly need about both eagle species, including where to see them, how to identify them and how to become involved in their conservation. Here are just a few.

www.snh.gov.uk/about-scotlands-nature/ species/recent-species-projects/sea-eagle
The website of Scottish Natural Heritage, with detailed information on both eagle species in Scotland.

www.white-tailed-sea-eagle.co.uk/
Excellent website dedicated to the White-tailed Eagle on Mull, with extensive information about the bird, plus advice on where to see it on the island.

www.cairngormsnature.co.uk/ golden-eagle
Helpful information about Golden Eagles and where to see them in the Cairngorms region.

www.forestry.gov.uk/forestry/goldeneagle
The website of the Forestry Commission, with information on both eagle species and their conservation status in Scotland.

animals.nationalgeographic.com/animals/birds/golden-eagle/
Extensive online resource from National Geographic, with information, images and video on the Golden Eagle

www.eaglefalconer.com/about.html
The website of falconer Alan Gates, with fascinating information and articles about his experiences training and flying Golden Eagles (see page 107).

youtube.com
A search will produce numerous video clips of both eagle species in action, including some dramatic amateur footage of hunting behaviour (plus, inevitably, some rubbish).

Satellite tracking online
You can follow the fortunes of satellite-tracked eagles online at the following websites
www.roydennis.org/satellite/
www.raptortrack.org/golden-eagle/
www.rspb.org.uk/discoverandenjoy nature/discoverandlearn/tracking/mulleagles/

Conservation

RSPB (www.rspb.org.uk/)
The RSPB is the country's largest nature conservation charity. They manage reserves around the UK to save birds, mammals and habitats.

Scottish raptor study group (www.scottishraptorstudygroup.org/whitetailedeagle.html)
A network of c. 300 raptor experts who monitor raptors in Scotland, including eagles, and have amassed an extensive and important database. Results are published annually as part of the award-winning Scottish Raptor Monitoring Scheme. New members are always welcome, and usually serve an apprenticeship with seasoned fieldworkers.

Wildlife Trusts (www.wildlifetrusts.org)
National conservation charity comprising 47 separate regional wildlife trusts across the UK, with information and advice on all aspects of British wildlife, and an extensive network of reserves – including some that are home to eagles.

Acknowledgements

I would like to thank all those whose help and encouragement lies behind this book. It was a pleasure, as always, working with the Natural History team at Bloomsbury and I am especially grateful to Julie Bailey for presiding over the excellent Spotlight series and inviting me onboard, and to my editor Alice Ward for her help, resourcefulness and patience – from the book's incubation to its fledging. Thanks, too, to Rod Teasdale for his excellent layout and design.

I would also like to thank all those naturalists and conservationists whose study of and concern for eagles over the years has brought us a deeper understanding of these birds and taught us how to live with them. Without their dedication, Britain's skies might now be an eagle-free zone.

On a personal note, I am especially grateful to Elspeth Macdonald and Roddy Paul, and their sons Alasdair and Ian, whose fine hospitality in wild Wester Ross has long given me the perfect base from which to head out in search of eagles. Many of my best eagle experiences have been in their company. And I would like to thank my own family: my parents, who encouraged my love of nature from the earliest days; and my wife Kathy and daughter Florence, with whom I have shared many memorable wildlife moments – not least with eagles.

Image credits

Bloomsbury Publishing would like to thank the following for providing photographs and for permission to reproduce copyright material.

While every effort has been made to trace and acknowledge all copyright holders, we would like to apologise for any errors or omissions and invite readers to inform us so that corrections can be made in any future editions of the book.

Key t = top; l = left; r= right; tl = top left; tcl = top centre left; tc = top centre; tcr = top centre right; tr = top right; cl = centre left; c = centre; cr = centre right; b = bottom; bl = bottom left; bcl = bottom centre left; bc = bottom centre; bcr = bottom centre right; br = bottom right

AL = Alamy; FL= FLPA; G = Getty Images; NPL = Nature Picture Library; RS = RSPB Images; SS = Shutterstock

Front cover t CORDIER Sylvain/hemis.fr/G, b Marcus Siebert/G; **back cover** t Colin Carter Photography/G, b Nature Picture Library/G; **1** © age footstock/AL; **3** Laurie Campbell; **4** Konrad Wothe/FL; **5** Ingo Arndt/FL; **6** Dr Peter Wernicke/G; **7** © Harry Eggens/AL; **8** Markus Varesvuo/NPL; **9** t SS, b SS; **10** t Mark Hamblin/G, b Chris Wallace/G; **11** Alarifoto/G; **12** Brian Southern; **13** Joseph Van Os/G; **14** John Fairclough/G; **15** Cathy Hart/G ; **16** Steven Ruiter/FL; **17** l © MAXPX IMAGES LIMITED/AL, r SS; **18** ImageBroker/FL; **19** Terry Andrewartha/FL; **20** Willi Rolfes/AL; **21** Brian Southern; **23** Willi Rolfes/AL; **24** Rainer Herzog/FL; **25** Bernd Zoiler/AL; **26** © AfriPics.com/AL; **27** Jose A. Bernat Bacete/G; **28** CORDIER Sylvain/G; **29** Public Library of Science; **30** Mike Unwin; **31** Mike Unwin; **32** t Bernd Rohrschneider/FL, b Wendy Dennis/FL; **33** SS; **34** Malcolm Schuyl/FL; **35** t John Hawkins/FL, b Joan Pollock/G; **36** SS; **37** Danita Delimont/G; **38** Mike Unwin; **39** t ImageBroker/FL, b Patrick Kientz/FL; **40** t Peter Giovannini/FL, b David Tipling/FL; **41** t Vincent Grafhorst/FL, b Gianpiero Ferrari/FL; **42** SS; **43** Desmond Dugan/FL; **44** Malcolm Schuyl/FL; **45** Malcolm Schuyl/FL; **46** Malcolm Schuyl/FL; **47** Guy Edwardes/G; **48** Mart Smit/FL; **49** Nature Picture Library/AL; **50** SS; **51** Jules Cox/FL; **52** t CORDIER Sylvain/G, c Thomas Maerent/FL, b Mike Unwin; **53** t Jules Cox/FL, c Derek Middleton/FL, b Mark Sisson/FL; **54** t ImageBroker/FL, b Mull Magic; **55** Mark Hamblin/G; **56** Ben Cranke/NPL; **57** Roger Tidman/FL; **58** Horst Jegen/FL; **59** Stefan Huwiler/AL; **60** SS; **61** SS; **62** Mike Unwin; **63** t MARKO KÖNIG/FL, b Willi Rolfes/AL; **65** SS; **66** David Tipling/FL; **67** Richard Costin/FL; **68** Dr Peter Wernicke/G; **69** SS; **70** SS; **71** Steven Ruiter/FL; 72 Tom Vezo/FL; **73** SS; **74** Robbie George/G; **75** Desmond Dugan/FL; **76** t © blickwinkel/AL, b Edwin Kats/RS; **77** © Nature Photographers Ltd/AL; **78** t Laurie Campbell/RS, b Laurie Campbell/RS; **79** Grzegors Lesniewski/FL; **80** t Desmond Dugan/FL, b ImageBroker/FL; **81** Mark Sisson/RS; **82** Michael Durham/FL; **83** Mark Hamblin/RS; **84** Jean-Francois Noblet/FL; **85** Peter Van Der Veen/G; **86** SS; **87** t Konrad Borkowski/FL, b Ian McCarthy/RS; **88** Nature Picture Library/G; **89** Daniel J Cox/G; **90** Education Images/G; **91** © Wildlight Photo Agency/AL; **92** t Mark Newman/FL, b Mark Hamblin/RS; **93** © Martin Thomas Photography/AL; **94** © Tom Kidd/AL; **95** t Chris George/AL, b John Eveson/FL; **96** David Hosking/FL; **97** ©RSPB Scotland Investigations Unit; **98** Timothy Allen/G; **99** De Agostini/G. Sosio/G; **100** t Duncan1890/G, b Stefano Tinti/SS; **101** DEA/G. GAGLI ORTI/G; **102** t SS, b SS; **103** Hulton Collection/G; **104** United StatesNavy; **105** DEA/M.SEEMULLER/G; **106** SS; **107** Alan Gates; **108** TTstudio /SS; **109** t Timothy Allen/G, b Timothy Allen/G; **110** Neil Lucas/NPL; **111** t © AF archive/AL, b Marc Tielesmans/AL; **112** Dan Kitwood/G; **113** Dan Kitwood/G; **114** Dan Kitwood/G; **115** t Paul Hobson/FL, b Michael Callan/FL; **116** Chris & Tilde Stuart/FL; **117** Peter Cairns/NPL; **118** Roger Tidman/FL; **119** l Dan Kitwood/G, r © age footstock/AL; **120** t Barcroft Media/G, b © Rebecca Cole/AL; **121** © Ashley Cooper pics/AL; **122** HEINZ HUDELIST/FL; 123 © Arco Images GmbH/AL.

Index